BARGAIN
ANTIQUES

BARGAIN
ANTIQUES

WINDWARD

Dedication

*To my parents who started it all, and
to Dave without whose help and
support it would never have been
finished.*

Editor: Donna Wood
Art Editor: Gordon Robertson
Designer: Steve Leaning
Production: Richard Churchill

Published by Windward, an imprint owned by
W.H. Smith & Son Limited
Registered No. 237811 England
Trading as WHS Distributors,
St John's House, East Street, Leicester LE1 6NE

© Marshall Cavendish Limited 1987

ISBN 0–7112–0474–8

Typeset in Century Old Style by Quadraset Ltd,
Midsomer Norton, Avon
Printed and bound in England by
Butler and Tanner Ltd, Frome

All estimated prices given in this book are correct
at the time of going to press. However, while every
care has been taken in the compiling of information
contained in this book, the publishers cannot accept
any liability for loss, financial or otherwise incurred
by reliance placed on the information herein.

Front cover top left: Novelty teapot of the 1930s
(The National Magazine Company Ltd); top right:
Woven bookmark (Mary Evans Picture Library);
bottom left: Coronet Midget 16mm Camera (Design
Council); bottom right: Clarice Cliff egg cup set
(The National Magazine Company Ltd).
Back cover top: Chad Valley Game Box 1915–1923
(Design Council); bottom left: Souvenir Handbag
Mirror; bottom right: Late Victorian brooch in
imitation ivory (all Design Council).

CONTENTS

INTRODUCTION

This book was written specially for the modest collector; the 'weekend' searcher who, although on a limited budget, enjoys visiting antique fairs and markets. For this reason, the items described are mostly of Victorian and later date, and they have been listed in straightforward A to Z format for quick reference. The book's handy size means it can be conveniently carried and consulted on the spot, whenever a possible bargain is found. A comprehensive index plus ample cross referencing throughout the text means that you need never miss the item you are looking for, and clear line drawings and photographs aid identification.

Special 'Bargain Buys' have been highlighted, showing how it *is* possible to pick up valuable antiques at low prices, providing you know where to look.

The industrial advances made from the early 1800s meant an increase in production levels, so the artifacts from this period are available to the modern-day collector more cheaply. The colourful and imaginative Art Nouveau and Art Deco pieces of the 1920s and 30s are also relatively inexpensive, and these are mentioned because they will be

Glass bottles from
the 19th century, p29

Susie Cooper
cup and saucer, p76

among the most coveted antiques of tomorrow.

Novice collectors are advised to follow a few simple ground rules. When buying glass, it is important to examine objects carefully for damage and restoration. Touch the piece with the eyes closed. This makes it easier to detect any chips or cracks. Damaged china will sound 'dead' if tapped lightly with a pen or pencil, lacking the resonance of perfect examples. The glaze should be inspected since restoration can never quite achieve the right finish. The parts most prone to damage are handles, teapot spouts, necks, and the hands and arms on figures. Staining on cheese dishes is not easily removable, nor is oven browning on meat dishes. Tea stains on cups, however, will usually bleach out. Rust spots on fabric are there for good, and check material closely for fine darns and holes by holding it up to the light.

Clocks should only be bought from a reputable dealer, as repairs can cost more than the clock itself. Check the number of strikes against the hour, and ensure the pendulum is not missing.

Jewellery should be examined under a bright light with a magnifying glass; with particular attention given to the claws on rings and the pins on brooches. Stones should be inspected closely for flaws, chips or cracks.

Veneer on wood should not be lifting as it cannot be stuck down adequately by the amateur. If mosaic pieces are missing on Tunbridgeware, these can be difficult to replace.

Damage is acceptable providing it enables a collector to purchase splendid but imperfect items cheaply. For example, a dark green claret jug in a pewter Art Nouveau stand was bought recently for only £10 because the glass was cracked. Undamaged, this would have sold for £120.

Auctions are a good source of bargains for collectors — but never buy 'blind'. Always view carefully first, as the rule of *'caveat emptor'* (let the buyer beware) applies. Other sources are antique fairs, flea markets, car boot sales, jumble sales, charity shops and junk stalls.

A Bacardi jug advertising rum. £15

ADVERTISING JUGS

Most bars and pubs today have a water jug on the counter, bearing the name of a product, such as Cutty Sark or Haig whisky.

The forerunners of these jugs were the advertising whisky jugs and flagons produced in the late 19th century, mainly for Scottish and Irish distillers with a keen marketing sense. They were usually made in brown stoneware with embossed or printed details on them. Occasionally they were coloured, sometimes in deep, mottled blue.

Doulton produced a flagon for Melrose Highland Whisky in 1875, and between 1883 and 1889 they made a range of these for John Dewar & Sons, adorned with Scottish landscapes and castles.

But it is the jugs that were produced from around 1930 onwards that provide the collector with the greatest bargains, as prices are still low. The distinctive red Haig jug made by Carlton Ware, for example, will cost around £15. Although these are still being made today, older pieces conform to a distinctive style.

Wade (makers of Vat 69, and J & B Scotch Whisky jugs), Burgess & Leigh, Wedgwood, Minton, and Royal Doulton (Claymore Whisky) all manufactured whisky jugs for different distillers. Some cost from £24 to £50, but many can be bought for between £8 and £15.

Right: Cigarette manufacturers also used jugs to advertise their wares, and a yellow Gold Flake jug will cost £20

AMERICAN OGEE CLOCKS

These weight-driven, striking clocks were designed originally as shelf clocks, although their large size (26 × 15 inches) would seem to make them more suitable for hanging. All examples found in Britain have a hole drilled in the back for the supporting nail.

The case is made of soft wood, usually pine, and veneered in rich, glowing mahogany. The glazed door is divided in two, the top half being clear, to show the dial, and the bottom half or 'tablet' decorated with pictorial scenes, flower motifs, or heraldic devices. There is sometimes also a transfer inscription, such as *Honi soit qui mal y pense* — 'Evil to him who evil thinks'. It is interesting to note that these mottoes are found occasionally printed back-to-front, as if applied in error.

The name ogee is derived from the 'S' shaped moulding, known as an ogive, which featured on the front of the case. Early shelf clocks had wooden movements, but the advent of rolled brass in the mid-1800s made the cutting of brass blanks for toothing and gearing simpler and more economical.

The first, and largest producer of ogees was Noble Jerome of Connecticut in 1839, and he was also the earliest manufacturer to use a brass movement in a 30-hour clock. He introduced two new features in clock design — a stiffening ridge stamped on to the rim of the wheels, and the count wheel strike — but the actual structure of the movement changed very little over the years. In 1840, the company changed hands, and in 1855 it was renamed the Newhaven Clock Company.

A mahogany-cased ogee with a scenic tablet and gilded surround. £75

Other makers included Seth Thomas, who began production in 1844; the Waterbury Clock Company; Birge Peck & Co, and Brewster and Ingrahams.

The clocks can be dated and identified with reasonable accuracy by various means — perhaps most helpful and interesting are the coloured tablets on the lower case doors. The earliest tablets were always of scenic content, sometimes showing specific places, such as the Burns Monument, or Views in Rome. Later tablets were decorated with flowers or fruit on plain backgrounds. Seth Thomas enclosed his central designs with an oval, while Westbury used a circular surround. Later Newhaven clocks have a central scene accompanied by highly ornamental gilt scrolling on the black surround. Mirrored tablets were employed early on, and Brewster and Ingrahams used etched glass.

The earliest dials were made of wood, with painted flowers in the corners, but by c.1850 sheet zinc was used instead. Dials displayed hands bearing a Maltese Cross after about 1860, and another feature to appear at this time was the embossed pendulum.

Accompanying papers and labels often provide important clues to the age of clocks. These were pasted originally on the inside of the case, with instructions on how to set up the clock, apply the oil, set the strike, and adjust the pendulum bob. If a Waterbury clock, for example, is found with instructions not to turn back the hands, then the piece can be dated to about 1874. Manufacturers' addresses are also useful indicators for dating specimens. Seth Thomas was based at Plymouth Hollow, but in the late 1860s the name of the town was changed to Thomaston in his honour. In addition, his labels were printed by Elihu Geer up until 1863, and then by Francis Loutrel — all helpful clues in determining the age of his clocks. Some papers showed a picture of the manufacturing factory, and these are interesting from an historical viewpoint.

Ogees by Chauncey Jerome, Bristol are particularly sought after and rare, being made only between 1840 and 1845.

Production of ogee clocks ceased around 1912, and only recently have they become collectable. A Jerome clock in good condition with a tablet showing the Burns Monument is catalogued at between £60–£100, but with diligent searching attractive ogees can be found for about £30.

ANNIVERSARY CLOCKS

Most people are familiar with anniversary clocks since they are often seen standing on a friend's mantelpiece or in the window of a jeweller's shop, with their four brass balls rotating backwards and forwards with fascinating regularity. But the anniversary clock has a long history, going back to 1841.

These clocks are also called 'torsion' or '400-day clocks'. The name torsion is derived from the twisting action of the pendulum bob, and the 400-day period refers to the length of time the clock will run without rewinding. Because of their popularity as birthday or anniversary presents, they are also known as 'anniversary clocks'.

The clock consists of a dial and movement supported on brass pillars, mounted on a circular brass base. The pendulum, usually four brass balls (or sometimes a heavy brass disc) is suspended on a very fine spring, the whole being protected by a glass dome.

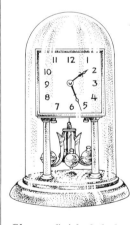

Chrome-finished clock with unusual square dial by August Schatz, Germany, 1936. £60

The majority of these clocks were made in Germany, and the first patent for a torsion pendulum clock was taken out in 1841 by Aaron Dodd. This model, however, was manufactured by the Year Clock Company of New York, and resembled an ogee clock. The traditional anniversary clock did not make its appearance until 1880 when the design was patented by Aaron Harder of Ramsen, Germany, and manufactured by the William Company of Frieburg, Silesia. In 1881, production was taken over by Gustav Becker, also of Frieburg. Other makers were Kienzle, and August Schatz (Jahresuhren-Fabrik). Apart from Claude Grivolas, a French manufacturer who took out patents in 1907, all the clock factories were in Germany.

The advent of World War I interfered with production, after which time clocks changed decoratively rather than technically. The climate improved in the 1920s and 30s, particularly after World War II when returning GI soldiers took examples of the clock back to America where a boom was created.

Anniversary clocks can be dated accurately, as indicated on the backplates which provide a great deal of information. After October 1913, clocks imported into the USA were required to have the words 'Germany' or 'Made in Germany' on the backplate. The serial number, patent number, and the name of the importer were often stamped here in addition. Occasionally, the name of the maker was also inscribed or stamped. Alterations in design are further aids to dating. A clock with a strike or bell, a type only briefly in production, can be dated to between 1880 and 1900. The lack of a spring guard, viewing aperture, or the addition of a 'crown' on the pendulum bob, all indicate early 20th-century manufacture.

A hooked (rather than pinned) suspension

spring is another feature of the period. Other changes in design included, early on, the introduction of four glass and oval style cases created by Claude Grivolas in 1824, and later the chrome-plated clocks produced by August Schatz in 1936.

Prices vary enormously, with early examples fetching more than £200. With diligent searching, however, anniversary clocks can be found from around £40–£50 upwards. Disc pendulum clocks command higher prices, but pendulum clocks on shabby brass bases can be cleaned up to reveal a sparkling finish. Clocks without domes are worth considerably less.

Arcadian China — see Crested China, page 86

ART DECO FACE MASKS

Brilliantly coloured and bizarre African masks were imported into Europe in the early 1900s and were soon highly prized by the artists and aesthetes of the day.

But it was in the 1920s that ceramic wall decorations came into vogue — from large wall plaques, to rows of flying ducks, and the Art Deco face mask, inspired by its African counterpart.

Nearly all face masks were of women, reflecting the 1920s preoccupation with the female form and face, although a few male examples were produced. The masks show the face in a highly stylized form, with slanting eyes, high cheekbones and well-defined lips. When makers began depicting famous film stars of the day, Marlene Dietrich was an obvious candidate, her features portraying exactly the exotic mood of the era. Other film stars were later immortalized, such as Rita Hayworth, sultry and languorous,

A typical face mask with a stylized 1920s hairstyle and, unusually, a canine companion. £75

A male face mask modelled on the famous crooner Bing Crosby. £90

and one collector has a mask of Bing Crosby hanging on his wall, complete with pipe.

The leading mask designer in England was Clarice Cliff (see: *Cliff, Clarice*) and she produced a great number. Some were modelled from life and portrayed faces of different nationalities. Royal Doulton also manufactured masks, but their faces are less stylized and more realistic, possibly less appealing. The complexions were natural and the finished effect rather doll-like.

The greatest exponent of ceramic masks was Goldscheider in Vienna and his pieces are highly sought after by collectors. Goldscheider preferred female faces, often placed against hands artistically extended, and modelled them to resemble Marlene Dietrich; the hair was formed of large curls of clay, the lips pouting and well defined, the eyes almost oriental.

A great many masks were not marked by their makers, especially Czechoslovakian examples. Colours were bold although sometimes the masks appeared in shades of cream or green, with the features unpainted. The hair styles echoed the fashions of the day, as did the hats, when worn. Some masks were made as wall pockets while others, in fine porcelain, were intended to be illuminated from behind.

Prices vary according to whether the masks are marked (or can be attributed to a well-known maker), and if the subject is identifiable, as with film stars or crooners.

Plain, self-colour examples can be found from about £40, but the price of a colourful and exotic mask is usually nearer £75. Examples by Clarice Cliff and Goldscheider are highly sought after and are now fetching several hundred pounds at auction.

BAKELITE

Originally used in the radio, car and electrical industries, this plastic was produced in the 1920s by the Bakelite Company in England, and the Bakelite Corporation in America. Bakelite is now a generic term for phenolic resin items.

This synthetic plastic first made its appearance in 1907 when a Belgian chemist, Leo Baekeland, discovered phenolic resin. Initially, the resin was hard and brittle but by adding fibres or woodflour it became more resilient. These ingredients also gave it the characteristic mottled finish. The most popular colours were black, dark brown, dark green, blue and red.

In 1924 experiments by Edmund Rossiter resulted in a water-white transparent moulding powder. This enabled a wider range of colours to be produced, and when used in combinations marbled and other striated effects could be achieved. 'Bandalasta' and 'Linga-longa' table-and picnicwares were manufactured in this material — commonly in shades of soft blue or pink marbled with white, and in strong flame

A yellow bakelite egg cup and cruet, the salt and pepper pot lids in the form of chickens' heads. £18

reds and yellows, also marbled. By 1932, however, new plastic materials were being produced (see: *Plastic*) and bakelite went out of favour.

The variety of bakelite and 'Bandalasta' articles made gives great scope to collectors, although prices have increased greatly. Ashtrays can be found in a number of shapes — round, oval, or square with chromed tops. Tea, coffee or tobacco canisters (with lids) are stamped with the name of the contents, and the decorative mouldings are pleasing. There are cups and saucers, beakers, plates, egg cups, teapots, napkin rings, candlesticks, cigarette cases, desk accessories, handbags, compacts — and many more items fashioned for both domestic and personal use.

Ordinary household items stamped 'Bakelite' will command prices from about £15 upwards, but in general, prices range from £5–£25 for an ashtray, and from £10–£20 for a decorative tea or coffee canister.

Bakelite jewellery has become increasingly popular and expensive in recent years. Brightly coloured brooches and clips in novel designs (yachts, prancing fawns, clowns' heads, flowers, etc) are usually priced from about £5–£35. Bangles and bracelets — either plain or moulded with rich floral and stylized patterns — are found from about £10–£40. Earrings, belt-buckles and necklaces (combined frequently with paste and chrome) are all sought after by Art Deco enthusiasts in America and Europe, and prices for these articles will continue to escalate.

Stylish handbags in colourful striated patterns with gilt-metal clasps and decorations, and novel cigarette cases (adorned, for example, with a hand opening the cover) are now fetching in the region of £100.

BARGE KETTLES

These Victorian items were made from a heavy brown glazed earthenware, and should not be confused with the metal items known as Bargeware, enamelled then brightly decorated by the bargee and his family (see: *Bargeware*). Other names for these earthenware vessels include 'long-boat ware', and Measham ware. The latter was made mainly in Derbyshire, and sold on the canal at Measham in Leicestershire.

The most common item in this range was the large teapot, known as a kettle because of its ungainly shape. The brown glaze was adorned with flowers in white, pink or blue, with the decoration appearing raised. Often, an inscription was included, placed within a panel or 'written' elsewhere on the teapot in white-coloured clay. Occasionally, the piece was dated (a boon for collectors), *eg. 'To Mrs Dobson 1885'*, or simply inscribed *'To A Good Friend'*. Names were mentioned frequently in the message, and it is likely that the kettles made popular gifts, given either in gratitude, or to commemorate an anniversary. The lids were sometimes fashioned in the form of miniature kettles themselves.

Sets of jugs, bowls and dishes were made, although these are rare today. The barge teapot or kettle was the favourite vessel, and prices for these range from £50 upwards, depending on the style of decoration, message and date.

The collector should not confuse antique pieces with the reproductions which are now being produced. These modern replicas are readily discernible, however, since their designs appear cruder, and somehow lack the naïve spontaneity of their Victorian counterparts.

A brown earthenware kettle bearing the message 'Remember Me', nicely decorated, and with an unusual finial to the lid. £90

BARGEWARE

A water can and handled bowl, brightly painted with flowers in primary colours. Between £20 and £40

Bargeware painting began on the narrow boats that used the canals up and down Britain, but by the mid-1880s the popular 'roses' and 'castles' were being used to decorate not only the boats, but some of the utensils found inside the barges.

Many of the domestic items were made of metal; jugs, buckets and pails, water cans and so on, and these were ornately painted, the whole surface of the object being covered with sprawling, brightly coloured flowers and leaves.

Perhaps the best known item is the 'Buckby' can — a water carrying can which was made in sizes ranging from 3 gallons to 8 gallons, the most usual size being of 4-gallon capacity. The can looked something like an upturned bucket, had a spout and a hinged lid. It was usually painted in dark green with a red band around the middle, the seams being picked out in yellow. The name of the bargee would often be added, or a motto such as, 'Trust To Me'.

The background was coloured according to the pattern chosen. Castles were always painted on a white background and incorporated into a scene with a bridge, lake, and mountains. Roses were painted in groups. Red petalled roses had a black background, yellow roses were on an orange background, while white roses stood out against pink. Other flowers such as pansies or daisies were used to fill in any spaces. Colours were always bright, flowers realistic.

Other patterns used were diamonds, hearts, sometimes elongated, anchors, compasses and a clover leaf. Occasionally a dog's head (perhaps the family pet?) would be incorporated into the pattern. The interior of the narrow boat, including the door panels, the table cupboards, drawer fronts and wooden stools were often decorated as well.

Canal ware is now being reproduced, so care must be taken. Prices vary but one can expect to pay from about £40 for a small to medium-sized water can, although a small, handled bowl was bought at an antique fair recently for £3, but in a rather battered condition.

BEADWORK

U nfortunately for present day collectors, much of the Victorian beadwork — the custom of sewing beads on to fabric and clothing — has disappeared. The fineness of the thread meant that items wore quickly, and few early pieces have survived. When used on clothing, the weight of the beads put a strain on the thread and material, and beads were often lost. Dresses of the 1920s and 30s, heavily bead-encrusted, are rarely found in first class condition for this reason. Well-preserved and stunning examples now cost several hundred pounds.

Initially, beads of coloured glass were used, and tubular 'bugles' which were made of clear glass. But by the end of the 19th century, jet (see: *Jet Jewellery*), coral, cut steel, seed pearls, silver (see: *Small Silver*) and gold beads were also in fashion.

Beadwork was used to decorate an infinite variety of objects including footstools, tea cosies, cushions and firescreens, and small personal possessions such as slippers, needle cases (see: *Etuis*) and pincushions, necklaces, belts, spectacle cases, book covers, watch pockets and fans (see: *Fans*) — all vividly embroidered with beads. These items,

A miser's purse made of metal beads and with a gilded clasp. £21

although often not in mint condition, can cost up to £100 depending on their quality of workmanship and appeal. Clothes such as dresses and jackets were adorned with jet beads, lending dignity to mourning garments, while shimmering metallic beaded designs were reserved for ball gowns.

Among the most prolific beadwork produced was that on purses and handbags. The miser's purse was made for gentlemen and consisted of a long 'sack', frequently beaded with cut steel and ornamented top and bottom with a tassel or fringe, gathered by a clasp halfway up. Beaded handbags were made in large numbers during the early 20th century, and display a variety of stunning effects. Flowers rioted in reds and greens across a pale background, or appeared in stylized fashion in pale colours sewn on to black. Geometric patterns were favoured during the Art Deco period featuring chevrons, stripes and squares, and traditional *petit point* embroideries were also revived. Some of the finest beadwork handbags of this era are those which display stylish clasps and chains in precious metals, ivory, tortoiseshell, silver and bakelite. The latter material was moulded frequently into fanciful, novel

A mahogany footstool, the beadwork slightly frayed at the edges. £70

forms, portraying exotic animals, stylized ladies and clowns, combined with superb beadwork below. Many of these bags, particularly those intended for evening use, were adorned additionally with long and colourful beaded fringes — similar in effect to the enormous bead necklaces worn by 'flappers' of the day.

Because of their decorative appeal, beadwork items are much in demand. Stools and firescreens will cost from about £50–£60 upwards, while purses and handbags can be found for about £20 in good condition. The most stylish 'period' example, however, can cost well over £50.

BELLEEK

The Belleek factory was founded in Ireland's County Fermanagh in 1863, after the discovery of a rich field of china clay and feldspar. Originally called McBirney and Armstrong, the factory later became known as McBirney & Co. A lustre glaze was added to the china, giving the characteristic pearl-like Belleek finish. The earliest wares were domestic, but by 1865 the factory was producing decorative pieces such as Parian figures (see: *Parian & Bisque*), portrait busts, floral-decorated openwork baskets, and the marine-inspired items so typical of Belleek. The china is very thinly potted, and light.

A variety of marks was employed by the factory, such as the impressed 'Belleek, Co. Fermanagh' which was used from 1863–90, and a harp motif with a crown above which appeared from 1863–80. The standard mark (first version), from 1863–91, shows a figurative group consisting of a seated hound, a tall tower, and a harp with the word 'Belleek' in a cartouche beneath.

☆ **BARGAIN BUY**
A small cream jug with green painted clover leaves, found at an antique fair for only £22

B

A posy holder with raised flower design and clover leaves on cream ground. £40

The standard mark (second version), from 1891 to the present day, shows a similar grouping but with the design partly enclosed by a ribbon-like banner containing the words 'Co. Fermanagh, Ireland'. The later marks are less detailed.

Prices for Belleek vary according to the item: Parian and basketwork items are expensive (from about £450 upwards), but small vases shaped like shells, and cups and saucers of marine design with an iridescent finish, can usually be bought for under £50.

BELLS - GLASS

If you are lucky enough to spot a slightly mauve or grey-tinged lightweight glass bell, with a shortish handle, snap it up at once. It is probably an early example of this popular collector's item, which is most frequently seen in shades of red, blue, opaque white and yellow. Purple glass bells are rare, and finely made specimens of lemon-yellow, orange and turquoise often fetch more than £60.

The demand for coloured glass in the early 19th century led to the mass-production of glass bells in numerous shades by the mid-1800s, with cherry red, or cranberry (see: *Cranberry Glass*), among the most popular. The bell itself was blown, with an opening reserved for the handle. When this was fitted, a loop of wire was also inserted from which to hang the pear-shaped clapper.

Some bells were of clear coloured glass, while others had latticino threads twisted through in fanciful patterns (see: *Paperweights*). But the handles provide the greatest variety, and appear of inverted baluster shape, or cut with geometric facets. Other handles feature an air twist running through them, or a tear drop bubble, while the most decorative examples have latticino threads spiralling from top to bottom.

More rarely, two-colour bells were produced, the handle being of one colour, the bell of another. Red and blue were combined effectively, as were cranberry and white, and turquoise and red. Sometimes coloured bells were adorned simply with clear glass handles. Clear colourless glass of sparkling 'white' tone may indicate recent manufacture, and such pieces should be avoided.

Bell collecting can be difficult since examples are not found in quantity at antique fairs. Specialists in old glass, however, are bound to have a few pieces in stock. Prices vary: plain coloured pieces dating from the late Victorian period start from about £40, while large and fanciful bells with decorative handles may cost somewhere in the region of £80–£100.

Late Victorian glass bell with clear handle and coloured bowl. £65

BLUE & WHITE TRANSFER PRINTED WARE

This was intended originally as a cheap alternative to hand-painted porcelain and china, and is now highly collectable. Previously, decoration on china and pottery was incised or painted by hand, but in the mid-1700s the process of printing in monochrome shades was tried and proved successful. The pattern was engraved on to copper plates which were then loaded with ink (prepared from various metallic oxides — in this case, cobalt for blue). A special kind of paper was pressed on to the copper sheets, picking up the design; the printed paper was then applied to the surface of the ware to be decorated, thus transferring the pattern. Black, underglaze-blue, red and mauve were the only colours that remained stable during firing, and cobalt-blue was most effective for its subtle variations in shade. 'Flow' or 'flown blue' was produced by allowing the colour to 'bleed' or flow slightly at the edges.

Chinese wares were popular during the 18th century and the oriental designs were imitated by numerous English factories (see: *Willow Patterned Ware*). By 1800, however, the fashion for recognizable European scenes and patterns superseded the *chinoiserie* styles of previous years.

The variety of 'blue and white' patterns is staggering and it is sometimes difficult for the beginner to know where to start. In addition, an enormous range of wares was produced in this style, which might further confuse the collector. Dinner and tea wares were made in quantity, and the new transfer-printing technique also appeared on washstand sets, feeding cups and bottles, tea kettles, smoker's sets, wine coolers, puzzle jugs,

A large meat plate in 'Wild Rose' pattern, named for its border. Printed in clear mid-blue. £70–£90

and even urine bottles. Among the most
collected items today are plates, and the
beginner would do well to concentrate on
these for their imaginative patterns, styles
and reasonable price ranges.

There was no copyright act until 1842,
and early engravers used scenes from
pattern and other illustrated books to
decorate their wares. Copeland & Garret
produced dinnerwares adorned with
scenes from a three-volume work on
Byron and his travels. Known as the
'Byron Views Series', these proved a
success.

Wedgwood's engravers copied floral
patterns from Curtis' Botanical Magazine,
and examples are now extremely
collectable, priced from about £50
upwards for a single plate.

In 1816 Spode introduced the 'Italian'
pattern which proved so popular that it is
still being produced today. This shows a
ruin on the left, a river, a tree on the
right, and figures and animals in the
foreground. Their 'Tower' pattern was
equally successful, featuring a bridge with
a tower over a river, with two men fishing
on the bank, and three birds in the
foreground.

Manufacturers copied each other's
designs and it is sometimes difficult to
ascertain from which factory the article
came. The 'Wild Rose' pattern, for
example, is credited to at least twenty
different factories. This shows a broad
river with two men fishing, surmounted
by a bridge having a cottage to the right.
A mansion is shown on the left of the
background, with a man standing in a
punt or shallow-bottomed boat in the
foreground. The scene was taken from an
engraving by W. Cooke of Nuneham
Courtenay, about five miles east of
Oxford. The name of the pattern, 'Wild
Rose', sometimes referred to as
'Improved Wild Rose', is derived from the

wide border of briar roses that surrounds the scene.

Sometimes wares are found with an all-over pattern. This was known as 'sheet-transfer', a process employed for its cheapness and ease of application since only one copper plate needed to be engraved. It was often used on toy dinner and tea services.

Small mugs, known as coffee cans (see: *Coffee Cans*) can make an attractive collection, and these may be bought for about £4 each, depending on the manufacturer.

Plates vary enormously in price, again depending on the manufacturer and the pattern, but attractive examples can be found from around £10 upwards, although early and rare examples will cost far more. Unmarked wares of 19th century origin tend to be cheaper than the prices mentioned above.

BOTTLES - GLASS

Presentation has always played an important part in the sale of food and drink, and in the early 1800s, glass was replacing pottery and earthenware as the ideal medium. There were some unscrupulous manufacturers in the provision industry at that time and many foods contained substances such as chalk and alum in flour, and dried leaves, such as blackberry, in tea. Green vitriol and copperas were added to beer to give it increased strength and a fine head. When the Victorians demanded that they should see the contents of the goods they were buying the new glass bottles became popular.

At first, the bottles were blown individually. A lump of molten glass would be gathered on to the long blow pipe, being supported on an iron pontil rod as the glass blower achieved the desired shape. The neck would be sheared off, leaving the bottle attached to the pontil rod. This was then broken off leaving a stump of irregular glass on the base of the bottle. Later, the pontil rod was pushed into the base before the final shearing, giving the bottle a characteristic indentation known as a 'kick up'.

Hinged moulds were also used in the early 1800s for making the body of the bottle, the neck and lip being applied afterwards, but it was not until *c.*1898 that the first entirely automatic machine for bottle-making went into production.

However, manufacturers still disliked the idea of the customer seeing exactly what was in the bottle, especially the makers of soft drinks, since their products contained large amounts of unsightly sediment. For this reason they favoured the use of coloured bottles, which were created by adding various amounts of iron oxide to the mix to produce the dark

Left to right: An Allenbury's baby's bottle in clear glass complete with box. £15. A dark brown mineral water bottle by Carruther's. £7. A small 'Crown' bottle in dark green glass bought for 20p, valued at over £30. A typical poison bottle in dark blue. £3

greens, browns and blacks now so familiar. By careful regulation of the furnace heat, and the judicious addition of copper oxide, emerald green, blue and various shades of red were also produced.

By using brass castings for the mouldings, it was possible to emboss the bottles, and traders were quick to exploit this for wholesale advertising. By the late 1800s seventy-five per cent of all bottles were embossed. Some were plainly marked with the name of the manufacturer of the contents, such as Bovril or Lea & Perrins; others had the name enclosed within a cartouche, accompanied by the emblem or insignia of the company. Even more elaborate was the design used by H. H. Warner of New York who marketed his patent medicines in bottles decorated with a heavily embossed safe, obviously using the play on words or symbols as a clever marketing technique. The embossing of bottles died out when new machinery was introduced to facilitate the applying of labels. This was cheaper and more efficient, although some manufacturers used both methods, such as Cobbold's Stout.

Beer and mineral waters posed a problem. Because of the gassy nature of the contents, bottles had to be provided with a stopper that wouldn't blow in transit or storage. William Hamilton introduced his egg-shaped bottle in 1841. This forced retailers to lay the bottle on its side, thus keeping the cork moist. It wasn't until 1887 that Hiram Codd came up with an alternative design. His solution was to insert a marble into the neck of the bottle. When filled, the gaseous nature of the liquid forced the marble hard up against a rubber seal, giving an airtight fit. With each bottle sold, a wooden cap and plunger was provided. The customer would then force the marble down into

A mineral water bottle in Codd style made in clear glass. £3

the neck of the bottle, where two glass lugs held it. The contents could then be poured out easily. Despite the arrival of the internal screw stopper in 1872, the Codd bottle survived until the 1930s.

Perhaps the best known of all bottles is the ribbed, dark blue or dark green poison bottle. Patent medicines were sold in a variety of bottles but all were distinctive in colour in order to avoid confusion. Medicine bottles are generally known as flats, ovals, rounds or panels, according to their shape. They were sometimes embossed with markers, indicating teaspoons or tablespoons. Babies' feeding bottles at this time were banana shaped, with a screw glass teat stopper.

The prices of bottles vary enormously, and it is almost impossible to give a guideline. A tour round an antique bottle fair will give the collector some idea of the wide range of prices, but jumble sales and flea markets will still yield bargains. A rare 'Crown' bottle was purchased recently for 20p — at a bottle fair it would cost £30; and a box of old bottles was bought at auction for only £1 and contained some prize specimens. The best advice for beginners is to read up on the subject, handle bottles to get a 'feel' for them, and visit antique markets. Knowledge, plus luck, are as necessary in this branch of collecting as they are in any other.

☆ **BARGAIN BUY**
An amber bottle heavily encrusted. Bought for only 50p because of its condition

BOTTLES - STONEWARE

D espite the upsurge of glass bottles in early Victorian times (see: *Bottles — Glass*), some manufacturers, namely ginger beer makers, resisted their use. There was a sediment in the mineral that

Left: A stoneware ginger beer bottle circa 1900. £8. Right: A stoneware flagon with two-tone body. £10

made ginger beer unattractive when displayed in glass, and so they preferred the discreet packaging of stoneware. These 19th century bottles featured internal screw stoppers, and transfer-printed labels and designs.

The majority of stoneware bottles were made by Doulton & Co (now Royal Doulton) and by Joseph Bourne at Denby, near Derby. All manner of items were produced, including hot water bottles, whisky, cider and gin bottles, meat and fish paste jars, ink and glue pots, and blacking pots. The firm of Pearson & Co manufactured stoneware mineral bottles as well as huge, six-gallon jars.

But it is the ginger beer bottle that offers the greatest scope for the novice collector. Initially, the labelling was cut or incised into the stoneware, but the fierce competition created by glass bottles, with their ornate embossing and decoratively moulded designs, led to transfer-printing being used on the ginger beer bottle to promote the contents. The manufacturer R. White stated on his bottles that their ginger beer had been 'unrivalled for 40 years'; the firm Ward's claimed their drink to be 'noted', and indeed they won a gold medal; while Down and Needham's was a 'celebrated home brew'.

Again, like glass bottles (see previous entry) prices vary, but a substantial and interesting collection can be built up from the less expensive pieces to be found at bottle fairs. Flea markets and boot fairs are good hunting grounds, too, as prices there are much cheaper. Many late 19th century stoneware bottles for ginger beer can be purchased in the £5–£30 range, with their contents and manufacturer's labels transfer-printed clearly across the front.

Examples which display glazed necks of contrasting colour are particularly attractive.

B

BREAD BOARDS
& ACCESSORIES

The Victorians, unable to leave anything plain and simple, carved and ornamented their bread boards with flowers and ears of wheat arranged decoratively around the circular or octagonal rims. These popular designs were combined frequently with mottoes and slogans such as 'Staff of Life' or 'Our Daily Bread', also carved elaborately on the rims. Breadboards were made invariably of pine, and an attractively carved example can cost £25 and more. Plainer pieces are usually priced from around £12 upwards.

Bread knives were made with blades of Sheffield steel (and if used today must always be dried immediately after washing, otherwise they will rust and discolour) with plain bone or carved wooden handles. It is often worth checking whether the bolster, between the handle and the blade, is hallmarked — since silver will increase the value.

Bread knives can be purchased for £2–£3 for plain, bone-handled varieties. Ornately carved wooden examples fetch over £30.

Bread plates, as opposed to bread-and-butter plates, are flat, china or pottery plates, slightly indented and rising at the edges. They are usually decorated with transfer-printed flowers and other stylized patterns, and can be most attractive when mounted on walls. Most are in the region of £6–£20.

Bread forks — the Victorians had an implement for everything — are wide, short, three-pronged forks with bone or ivory handles and silver bolsters, and were used for passing the bread around the table. These cost from around £8.

A Victorian bread board carved with ears of wheat and the inscription 'Our Daily Bread'. £25

BRISTOL GLASS

This type of coloured lead glass was produced by factories in the Bristol area and elsewhere in England from c.1760–1825. Blue was the most popular colour, created by the addition of cobalt oxide to the mix to achieve the intensely rich blue so characteristic of this type of glass. Other colours were also produced: brilliant deep green, amethyst, and more rarely yellow and dark red.

Two Victorian wine glasses in deep blue and green. £30 each approximately

Some of the wares, such as goblets, were gilded with Greek 'key-fret' patterns around the rims, while others were decorated by cold-painting and enamelling with fruit and floral motifs. Wine glasses, bowls and pickle jars were adorned frequently in this manner, in colours such as red and blue. Decanters and cruet sets often featured gilded 'name' plaques, in imitation of wine and condiment labels.

Late 18th century pieces are rare and beyond the pocket of the average collector. Wine glasses of a later date, however, in deep blue or green, can be purchased singly for about £20–£40 each and built up into an attractive collection. These harlequin sets make splendid displays, particularly when laid out on the dining table for formal supper parties.

Small, early 19th-century mustard pots and jugs can also be found at modest prices at antique fairs and markets at specialist stalls.

BUCKLES

For anyone with a limited amount of display space, buckles are ideal to collect as they look well arranged in a box-type frame hung from the wall.

Shoe buckles became fashionable at the time of Charles II but by the end of the 19th century they had gone out of vogue. During this period they were made of silver, pewter, enamel, mother-of-pearl, and steel.

Belt buckles were immensely popular in Victorian times and were made in a variety of materials: gilt or silver filigree, cut steel, mother-of-pearl, gold, pinchbeck (a copper and zinc alloy that resembled gold), tortoiseshell, 'French jet', bone and ivory. Some were decorated with paste stones, beadwork and seed pearls. Coiled snakes or serpents were fashionable at the time, and these exotic motifs appeared frequently on buckles. Silver was chased, engraved, or embossed and large buckles were made in ornate and twisted patterns.

The majority of large silver buckles were made in Birmingham from the late 18th century onwards, and these elaborate examples are often bought today as gifts for nurses on passing their final exams.

In the Art Nouveau period, from about 1890 to 1910, buckles featured maidens' heads with swirling hair, butterflies and peacocks. Large buckles adorned the backs of dresses, and were made of coloured paste or silver.

The 1920s and 30s saw the emergence of sharply geometric designs and bold colours. Enamelled buckles in bright red, green and blue fastened the belt at the waist or hip. Plastic buckles were mass-produced in a variety of shapes and colours, all designed to make an impact. Large black plastic buckles were dramatic, and plain colours were enlivened by the addition of metallic silver resembling fish scales. Novelty pieces were also created in the form of large flowers, fawns and elephants.

Buckles of the Victorian era and later are still comparatively cheap. Plastic buckles are usually priced under £10,

Ornate cut steel belt buckle made in the 19th century. £22

Pinchbeck shoe buckle with embossed decoration. £18

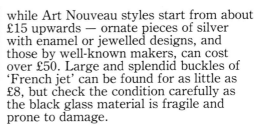

Ivory buttonhook with shoehorn-style handle. £12

while Art Nouveau styles start from about £15 upwards — ornate pieces of silver with enamel or jewelled designs, and those by well-known makers, can cost over £50. Large and splendid buckles of 'French jet' can be found for as little as £8, but check the condition carefully as the black glass material is fragile and prone to damage.

BUTTONHOOKS

E legant implements for undoing rows of tiresome buttons, buttonhooks have become a popular collector's item. The handles offer an infinite variety, and were made in every conceivable material, shape, design and pattern.

Buttonhooks vary enormously in size, from about 20 inches long, to three quarters of an inch for a glove hook. The shanks were nearly always steel, to cope with the tough leather, although tiny glove hooks can be found with gold or silver shanks.

Silver buttonhooks (see: *Small Silver*) were made mostly in Birmingham and from their hallmarks these can be dated accurately, although sometimes the mark is concealed cleverly in the ornate design. The most productive period was between 1860 and 1925 when buttoned boots and shoes were fashionable, although the history of buttonhooks goes back to the beginning of the 17th century. The buttonhooks usually formed part of a dressing table set, along with brushes, combs and mirrors, and can be found decorated with cherubs' heads, feather patterns and scrollwork embossing. Novelties weren't neglected either, and buttonhooks were made with swan's head handles, dogs, owls, cats, fish and reptiles, mostly in silver. Buy these if you see them below £25, as their value is likely to escalate rapidly.

Other materials were used, too. Ebony buttonhooks, always plain, were produced to match the ebony toiletry sets that graced the dressing table. Ivory, bone, wood and horn were also employed. Tunbridgeware examples are rare and expensive — anything below £50 is a bargain. Mother-of-pearl hooks were popular and the shell was carved and cut in various shapes and patterns, including the 'candle-end' and 'featherhead' styles. These are found frequently, and are reasonably priced.

Buttonhooks with handles of precious and semi-precious stone, such as agate, amethyst, cornelian and bloodstone, make attractive additions to a collection, with their colourful banded effects. Glass-handled examples also provide a splash of colour, with deep green or amethyst showing to advantage.

Early plastic made its appearance in the Victorian era (see: *Plastic*) and imitations of ivory, tortoiseshell and amber were produced. In the 1920s and 30s vivid colours and outrageous designs, such as handles in the form of female legs, made their appearance. Many items of this era sell for under £10, although more unusual designs are nearer £20.

Folding buttonhooks were made by steel makers to appeal to the male market. They were ideal for hanging on a watch chain, or slipping into the pocket for carrying about in case a change of footwear was necessary. Penknives, featuring blades, a corkscrew and buttonhook, were also made. A dual purpose buttonhook-cum-shoehorn was produced in the 1920s and 30s, known as ladies' purse or pocket companions. These were sometimes encased in leather holders, and make a valuable addition to any collection.

Victorian silver-handled buttonhook, ornately embossed. £25

Plain 'advertisement' buttonhooks were issued with the trader's name stamped or embossed on the looped handle, and all manner of goods were advertised in this way.

Silver buttonhooks will cost from about £20 upwards, depending on their condition and design, but tinier glove hooks in silver, designed to tackle the long, minutely buttoned kid gloves of the fashionable Edwardian lady, are more expensive. Plain ebony hooks are about £8–£10, as are later examples in plastic. Those in mother-of-pearl are priced from about £7 upwards.

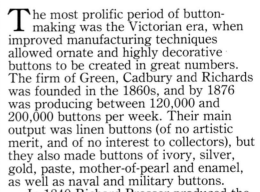

BUTTONS

A 19th-century celluloid button resembling ivory. £4–£5

The most prolific period of button-making was the Victorian era, when improved manufacturing techniques allowed ornate and highly decorative buttons to be created in great numbers. The firm of Green, Cadbury and Richards was founded in the 1860s, and by 1876 was producing between 120,000 and 200,000 buttons per week. Their main output was linen buttons (of no artistic merit, and of no interest to collectors), but they also made buttons of ivory, silver, gold, paste, mother-of-pearl and enamel, as well as naval and military buttons.

In 1840 Richard Prosser produced the first porcelain button in Birmingham, while working for the Minton factory. He held the monopoly until about 1850 when the French manufacturers copied him and produced ceramic buttons in great numbers. Prior to this, during the early 1800s, the firm of Josiah Wedgwood made buttons in salt-glazed earthenware, and in the famous blue jasperware with fine decorative relief designs in the neo-classical style. These are highly prized by collectors, and are now quite scarce.

Glass buttons were made in England as far back as the late 1600s, but it is the period from the mid-1800s that produced some of the best examples. Black glass ones (also described as French jet) are very collectable and come in a variety of smooth and faceted styles. Coloured glass buttons sometimes featured idyllic scenes and landscapes, flowers, and portraits of women mounted within the glass itself. Paperweight buttons were modelled on the millefiori ('thousand flowers') cane pattern, although complete sets are rare, and will cost well over a hundred pounds. Odd ones, however, from which interesting 'harlequin' sets can be formed, can be purchased for a few pounds.

Mother-of-pearl buttons were made in their thousands. Plain ones are too numerous to have any real value, but intricately carved and decorative sets are prized. Sometimes a mother-of-pearl button was set in a metal mount, especially during the Art Nouveau period (approximately 1890–1910) and these are sought after. Art Nouveau buttons were sometimes made of silver, but mostly of stamped metal. These were adorned frequently with portraits of women with long, flowing hair, or swirling floral designs. Many featured Sarah Bernhardt, the French actress of the period, and such examples are highly prized.

Cut steel buttons, being durable, may be found in plentiful supply today, and make a good starting point for the beginner. Sometimes they were filigree-decorated, or lacquered, and occasionally embellished with paste stones. The cut steel facets were also used in combination with wood, brass and other metals, as well as ivory, bone and mother-of-pearl.

Enamelled buttons were made as early as the 16th century, but most found today date from the late 19th and early 20th centuries. These are extremely decorative, in pastel or bold colours displaying exquisite flower paintings and, in the 1920s–30s, abstract and geometric patterns were created by many of the Birmingham factories. Enamel buttons in excellent condition are at the top end of the market when it comes to price, although Art Deco sets in silver or gilt-metal can sometimes be purchased for under £50. Due to the fragility of the enamelled surface, many pieces are worn or damaged, and are best avoided.

A new area for the collector is the bakelite or plastic button which was produced from *c.*1870 onwards. Colourful Art Deco examples, and the fanciful styles of the 1940s, are sought after by collectors of these periods — but many sets are still reasonably priced, from £5 upwards. Bakelite and celluloid buttons can be displayed spectacularly when re-sewn onto modern clothes and accessories.

Wooden buttons are mostly of 19th and 20th century origin, although this material had been used for centuries. Mauchline buttons (see: *Mauchline Ware*) are prized, as are those from Spa in Belgium. These were painted buttons (usually with flowers), protected by a thin coat of varnish, and are either round or oval in shape. Other wooden buttons were carved or inlaid with mother-of-pearl or metal. During the 1920s and 30s, wooden buttons were used extensively for children's clothing, and were decorated with amusing pictures.

Plastic buttons cost about 50p each, while cut steel examples are priced anywhere between 50p and £5, depending on their age, condition and design. Ceramic buttons may cost more, and a china button with a pretty floral decoration was found recently for £15 at an antique fair.

CADDY SPOONS

These were used from *c.*1770 onwards to transfer the tea leaves from the caddy to the teapot. They can be found in silver and silver plate and, in the 20th century, examples were also made in chrome. Although the latter are not yet highly regarded by collectors, one day they will be prized, as many bear the crest of the town where they were bought as souvenirs.

One of the most popular and early designs for caddy spoons was the shell-shaped bowl, and there exist an infinite number of variations on this simple theme. Other bowl shapes took the form of thistles, shovels and leaves — either plain, embossed, pierced or with filigree designs, accompanied by highly decorative handles. The filigree and pierced work was designed to allow the dust and very fine tea leaves to fall through, so as not to enter the pot and spoil the brew. As filigree shapes are not always recognized as caddy spoons, these are worth looking out for since their prices might be lower. The filigree surface — covering the bowl and handle of the spoon — left little room for a hallmark, and as such these pieces are frequently cheaper than their marked silver counterparts.

Caddy spoon handles were of silver, silver-plate, bone or ivory, but the latter were usually reserved for scoop-shaped spoons.

A caddy spoon can sometimes be dated (apart from the hallmark on silver examples) by the initials which were engraved occasionally on the handle or bowl. By examining the calligraphic style of the lettering, it is sometimes possible to deduce the period when the spoon was made. It is most important to check the

An early caddy spoon from about 1800 with typical shell-shaped bowl in silver. £35

condition of silver caddy spoons. The silver is soft and prone to split, especially if the spoon has been in regular use for a great many years. Look out, too, for a 'marriage' — that is where the handle has been welded on to another bowl. Careful examination will show the joining line and, if present, this will decrease the value. All silver spoons were hallmarked, and a full, clear stamp will add to the price.

Silver-plated caddy spoons cost a great deal less than silver ones, and can be found for around £8, but check the condition of the plating. If worn or yellowed in appearance, it is better left alone. Plain silver spoons will cost from about £15 upwards, depending on the date. In general, the earlier the spoon, the more it will cost. Elaborate and heavily cast examples are priced from about £70 upwards, and can be found in antique markets, fairs and at small specialist silver shops.

CAMERAS

It wasn't until about 1880 that photography became a popular pastime, due to the availability of dry plates. Previously, wet plates had been used and the photographer had to sensitize these in the dark and, after the photograph had been taken, develop and fix them himself. Another boost for the do-it-yourself camera buff was the development of flexible film by George Eastman (founder of Kodak) a few years later, with his promise, 'You press the button, we do the rest'. This eliminated the need for self-processing and developing.

Collectable cameras, manufactured after the late 1800s, fall into three categories: the folding bellows camera, the box camera, and the small bakelite-cased camera. It has been estimated that over 30,000 different types of camera were produced from the end of the century to 1939. Many examples, however, have become increasingly difficult to find for purchase.

Zeiss Box-Tengor camera circa 1938. £18 in good condition, although can be cheaper at antique fairs

Early Kodak cameras were simple black boxes, with the shutter operated by a string. Slightly later models of these can be found for about £5 or £6. Coloured boxes covered in red, green or blue leatherette increase the price by about £2.

Kodak cameras are an area which the beginner would do well to explore, as the company also produced quality 35mm cameras in the 1940s and 50s, such as the Retina and Retinette — both of which are available in great variety, and can still be used. The Kodak range of cameras was vast, offering an opportunity for research by the collector.

Folding cameras with bellows are also cheap, costing about £7 or £8, but it is important to check that the bellows are not torn or damaged in any way. The lenses in early wooden box cameras are sometimes missing, so careful examination is necessary.

The 20th-century bakelite or plastic-cased camera is well worth looking out for. Prices start from about £2, and examples of this type are plentiful.

Antique cameras should be purchased from dealers specializing in photographic items. Their enthusiasm and advice will prove helpful for the beginner. Also, if planning to use the camera, check that the film size is still available from photographic dealers and shops.

CANDLE SNUFFERS & WICK TRIMMERS

Top: Silver-plated Victorian wick trimmer (without a tray). £20. Bottom: A steel wick trimmer of plain style. £9

These will no doubt puzzle the novice, since snuffers resemble a pair of scissors with a small box on top, or at the side. But these implements had a specific use in homes from the 15th century onwards. Candles were made largely of tallow, and burnt down more quickly than the loosely twisted wicks. As a result, the wicks were a source of danger and collapsed if they got too long, falling smouldering on to the table. The guttering wick was therefore trimmed, using the candlesnuffers as scissors, so that the unwanted part of the wick fell safely into the box.

The snuffers were made in silver, brass, silver-plate and steel, sometimes accompanied by a tray with elaborately scrolled or pierced borders. The style of the 'scissors' altered little from period to period, although the handles were sometimes ornamented by loops. The lidded box was usually placed on top of the blade part, and was of narrow oblong shape. Occasionally, it was mounted on the side of the blade, left curved and open. Steel versions are still cheap and can be bought for around £8, although the addition of a tray will more than double their value. Early 19th century examples of silver-plate will cost from about £20.

Candle extinguishers appeared as bell-shaped snuffers, often made of ceramic and in novel designs. Royal Worcester produced a great many, modelled with portrait busts of men, women and girls, or sometimes with complete figures, such as a nun with a wide-brimmed hat, carrying a prayer book and rosary, or a small girl with a bell-like skirt. These are now priced at about £80, although modern reproductions from the factory are considerably less — and represent a new area for the collector, as these pieces are destined to become the collectables of the future.

Some extinguishers were of simple cone form, and came complete with a saucer or tray. Others, in brass or copper, were shaped like bells with a ring at the top for easier handling. Souvenir examples were made by W. H. Goss and other makers of crested china, and are more easily found for purchase than other ceramic types. Prices vary between £30 and £50 depending on age, condition, rarity and appeal.

CANDLESTICKS - METAL

With the introduction of new mechanized processes in Victorian times, brass candlesticks (among other domestic wares) were turned out in their thousands. This mass-production resulted in cheaper prices — and indeed, many surviving examples of 19th-century origin remain reasonably priced today. Whereas a pair of George II candlesticks would cost hundreds of pounds, a similar Victorian pair can be bought for between £40 and £60 — making pieces of this period accessible to the collector of modest means. Oddly enough, Victorian candlesticks escaped many of the over-ornate rococo styles so characteristic of mid-19th century tastes, perhaps because manufacturers were preoccupied with the design of the new-fangled oil lamp.

Victorian brass, as opposed to modern brass, is of a lighter colour, and early examples may appear of pale tone. When purchasing candlesticks, it is important to check that there has been no welding or soldering to any part, and that there are no breaks in the metal. Modern reproductions in brass are now being made, and can be 'distressed' by denting and scratching the surface in an effort to make them appear old. Candlesticks should be turned upside down to examine the screws, if any, and to check the underside of the brass for newness. Some sticks were fitted with plungers that allowed the candle to be forced up as it burned lower, and this is a sign of age. Single brass candlesticks are much cheaper than pairs and a typical Victorian example can be found for about £20. A pair would cost £50–£60.

Silver-plated candlesticks imitated the silver versions found on the rich man's table, and were in vogue from the mid-1700s when the Sheffield plate process of fusing silver on to copper was invented. But when George Elkington introduced his new method of electro-plating in 1840, plated candlesticks came within everyone's reach. Branched candelabra were also fashionable at this time and copies of elaborate silver versions were made. An early two-

A pair of late Victorian candlesticks with attractively-shaped stems. £45

branched candelabra of *c*.1850 will cost about £50, and a single stick about £20–£30.

Pewter was favoured by late 19th century craftsmen, in keeping with the hand-finished effects of the Arts and Crafts style, and the flowing lines of Art Nouveau. Examples in this metal are sought after today and can cost from £30 upwards. Those created by Liberty and Co in their well-known 'Tudric' range, and pieces adorned with bright enamelling, are now fetching several hundred pounds at auction.

Chambersticks were candleholders of brass or other metal, having a short holder set on a saucer-like base to catch any drips of candle grease lost when carrying the candle to bed at night. Sometimes there was a cone-shaped snuffer set at the side of the saucer. Late 19th-century chambersticks were sometimes made of enamel, and these can be purchased cheaply for about £5. When checking condition, make sure the enamel isn't chipped or damaged. Brass chambersticks will cost about £20, depending on their condition and age.

CANDLESTICKS - GLASS & CHINA

N othing enhances the flame of a candle quite like glass, but it wasn't until the advent of pressed glass (see: *Press Moulded Glass*) that glass candlesticks were available to the masses. Clear coloured glass was used by the Stourbridge glassmakers in shades of red, blue, a sharp greeny-yellow, dark green and amber. Because the moulding process proved so versatile, candlesticks could be adorned with many patterns and designs

— from simple, plain and elegant styles, to those with ribbed columns, and baluster shapes with basketwork feet. The variety of design and decoration was enormous.

At the turn of the century, trinket or toiletry sets came into vogue (see: *Trinket Sets*) and these were made with matching candlesticks for ladies' dressing tables, in china, glass and ebony.

Because pressed glass was cheap, candlesticks of this type were plentiful — and large numbers have survived intact for collectors today. A single glass candlestick may cost only £5 or £6, while a pair might be priced from £15–£18. Attractively coloured pieces tend to be more expensive, such as those of slag or cloud glass which might cost from about £35 each. Chips and cracks will decrease the value, so it is important to examine pieces carefully, especially ornate examples in glass.

China candlesticks have always been popular, particularly during Victorian times when advanced manufacturing processes made them affordable to everyone. Floral patterns were favoured, especially roses. Some early Victorian candlesticks had metal 'pricks' on to which the candles were impaled. Since the shaft was hollow, the candle could be pushed firmly on to the prick, and forced down the stem. As the candle burned lower, the prick could be pushed up by means of a metal rod, thus extending the life of the candle. China candlesticks compare in price to those of glass, although prices are rising.

In the 1920s, cheap china articles were imported into England from Japan in large quantities, and some very ornate candlesticks can be found from this period for between £12 and £25. Noritaké is a good name to look out for (see: *Noritaké China*).

☆ **BARGAIN BUY**
Left: A continental candlestick in the form of a cherub. This has some restoration and cost only £15.
Right: A Grimwades Winton ware candlestick decorated with pink roses, made in the 1930s and found at a flea market for £2

CARD CASES

W henever upper class Victorians paid a social call, they carried their engraved visiting cards with them. The cases they used to hold their cards measured about three by four inches, and were made of various materials: ivory, pâpier maché, tortoiseshell, wood, leather, gold, silver, and mother-of-pearl.

Silver examples are sought after and can cost around £30 upwards. They were plain, embossed or engraved elaborately with floral and geometric patterns, often accompanied by the owner's initials or monogram. Some were engine-turned, a cheaper method of engraving. Examples were usually hallmarked under their lids, on the inside rims, so as not to detract from the exterior designs.

Wooden cases were frequently inlaid with coloured woods or mother-of-pearl, perhaps made of Tunbridgeware or Mauchline ware, and bought as souvenirs (see: *Tunbridgeware* and *Mauchline Ware*). Ebony cases were always plain, the only ornament being a simple silver shield or plaque on to which the initials of the owner could be engraved. These were usually purchased by widows in mourning.

Mother-of-pearl was used extensively for card cases, sometimes in a chequer-board pattern, or in conjunction with tortoiseshell and silver.

Tortoiseshell cases, with their mottled surfaces ranging in tone from creamy yellow to dark brown, appeared in plain or fancy styles. Elaborate examples were inlaid with a tracery of leaves and other delicate patterns in contrasting pearl, silver or gilt-wire. Due to the material being fragile, many tortoiseshell cases have been damaged over the years. Perfect and ornate examples are hard to

Top to bottom: Brass card case ornately engraved and in fine condition £35–£40; Cedarwood case with ivory studding and banding £50; simple wooden card case with a pattern of leaves painted in subdued colours £25

49

find, and usually cost from £40 upwards.

Expensive cases (other than silver) were frequently velvet-lined. When buying ivory or tortoiseshell, make sure the surface isn't rubbed or scored. A nice finish is essential for a good collection.

Plainly veneered tortoiseshell cases, as opposed to the decorative ones mentioned above, and those of mother-of-pearl, fetch from about £20–£30 at auction, while those of ebony might realize something in the region of £8–£12.

CARLTON WARE

The factory making Carlton Ware began life in 1890 under the name Wiltshaw & Robinson. It was not until 1957 that the firm's title was changed to Carlton Ware Ltd, and it is the items produced from 1925 onwards that collectors are most interested in.

The lustre ware produced in the late 1920s is highly sought after (see: *Lustre Ware*). Vases, ginger jars, small dishes and ornaments were made in dark blue, leaf green and a rich red known as 'Rouge Royale'. These were beautifully decorated and painted before the lustre glaze was added. Birds are shown with long sweeping tails, with tiny dots of paint resembling jewels among the gilded foliage. Lustre ware ranges in price from about £40 to £70.

Perhaps more appropriate for those on a limited budget are the pretty floral ceramic items dating from the 1940s. These include jam pots, small sweetmeat dishes, cruets, toast racks, cheese dishes, cream jugs, sugar bowls, cups and saucers. Some are modelled in the form of foxglove or primrose leaves with the appropriate flower, and come in pale yellow or green. Small jam dishes appear

50

A selection of Carlton Ware from the 1930s, prices ranging between £12 for the toast rack, £18 for the dish with foxglove pattern, and £40 for the house-shaped sugar shaker

frequently as pink daisies with yellow centres. Also common are the green lettuce-leaf dishes, bearing a scarlet tomato in relief. These have matching cruet sets, sometimes with salad bowls and servers. More unusual are the long celery dishes with matching plates. These colourful domestic wares are found at antique markets and fairs, and usually cost from about £12 to £15 each.

Small items of Carlton Ware can be found in pastel colours, decorated with flowers in a deeper, contrasting tone. These are usually highly glazed, and date from the 1950s — and are not yet as sought after as earlier pieces. As a result, prices are low and a small, boxed jam dish with matching spoon can be purchased for £8–£10.

CAR MASCOTS

It is believed that the figure of St Christopher, once the patron saint of travellers, was portrayed on some of the earliest car mascots, and records show that when Lord Montagu of Beaulieu drove his car to the House of Commons in 1899, the radiator cap was adorned with a statuette of that saint. A winged wheel graced the bonnet of an Austin Grand

*Amusing policeman
mascot in chrome. £70*

Prix racing car in 1908, and by 1910 mascots were available to motorists everywhere.

Apart from their decorative appeal, there were other reasons for the car mascot. Early cars were fitted with calorimeters — a device for registering the water temperature in the radiator to prevent it from boiling over. These were mounted on the radiator caps on the bonnet and soon became decorative. Automobile clubs also seized the opportunity for a bit of free advertising by issuing mascots bearing their emblems. The AA is believed to have been the first to issue one as early as 1905.

Symbols of luck and good fortune were popular, and black cats, pixies and elves were common mascot subjects. Around 1910 humorous pieces were also produced, including revolving traffic policemen, and Mickey Mouse appeared from about 1920.

Rolls-Royce, a superior car, featured an elegant mascot (probably the most easily recognized in the world) — the 'Spirit of Ecstasy'. Designed by Charles Sykes in 1911 this mascot went on to win a gold medal in 1920. The French took to mascots with great enthusiasm, and René Lalique, the famous glassmaker, produced some outstanding examples. The eagle's head, fierce and predatory, was well known, and in the 1920s 'Victoire' was made, showing a girl's head with the hair streaming out in the wind in typical Art Deco style. Girls, both dressed and nude, and animals such as prancing horses were extremely popular.

The use of glass gave a new dimension to mascots. According to one advertisement '. . . it reflects the light of approaching cars and appears to really flame'. Sometimes the mascots were hollow for the insertion of a light bulb, so they could be used as parking lights.

Coloured filters were also employed to
change the colour of the light to match
that of the car, and sometimes a rainbow
effect was achieved. The Red Ashay
company produced a four-colour filter
which, when used with a propeller
system, altered in shade according to the
speed of the engine. These novel effects
appeared frequently on their range of
female mascots, such as the 'Butterfly
Girl' and 'Vitesse' model (inspired by
Lalique).

Mascots took many shapes. Girls, fish,
animals, birds, tortoises, lizards and frogs,
comic characters, aeroplanes, and even
the head of a Red Indian — anything and
everything was mounted on the bonnet of
a fashionable car, and all are highly prized
today.

For collectors, there is a wide range to
choose from. Well-known mascots such as
the 'Spirit of Ecstasy' or 'Victoire' have
achieved incredibly high prices (over
£500), but there is still scope for the more
modest pocket. Mascots were made of
moulded glass, metal (such as chrome,
brass and silver-plate), wood, and
even porcelain but aren't always
recognizable as such, statuettes and
figures having been converted into
paperweights, book ends, or lamps. It is
possible to recognize this adaptation,
however, since any ornament fixed on to
the radiator cap would have been fastened
by using a wide bolt at its base, if the
fixing bolt is small, the figure would
probably not have been a car mascot. So a
bargain might be found where least
expected.

Metals can give a clue to age, as the
mascot was made to match the metal of
the radiator grille. Early mascots were
usually brass, followed by bronze, nickel
and chromium-plate. Styles became more
streamlined as time went by, reflecting
the shape of the car itself. So, square

chunky mascots are earlier in date than those of aerodynamic form. Art Deco mascots are easily recognized for their stylized, elongated forms emphasizing the period obsession for speed and travel.

Chrome-plated mascots can be purchased for as little as £15–£20, while early brass examples are more likely to be found in the region of £30 upwards. Humorous mascots, such as revolving policemen, and silver-plated figurines will cost about £60 upwards.

CARNIVAL GLASS

Top: Dark green 'Grape and Cable' patterned dish. Made by both Fenton and Northwood. £25. Bottom: The rare three-footed dish in 'Wishbone' pattern will cost £100

This pressed mass-produced glass with a shimmering iridescent finish, reminiscent of Tiffany glass (and sometimes called 'poor man's Tiffany'), was first made in the United States between 1907 and 1928. It got the prefix 'Carnival' when second-rate glass was offered as prizes at funfairs and carnivals.

The Fenton Art Glass Co introduced the first carnival glass and called it 'Rubi-glass'. This was quickly followed by 'Golden Iris' from the Northwood Glass Co, and in 1910 the Dugan factory went into production. The Millersburg Glass Co and the Imperial Glass Company were the other big American manufacturers.

The iridescence was obtained by spraying the pressed glass with a variety of metallic salts, then re-firing it to give this a lustrous, 'oil-on-water' finish. This special colouring was applied to both dark and light glass. Selenium orange applied to clear glass was the most popular shade, sometimes called 'Marigold' and graduating in tone from a pale orange to a fiery flame-like intensity. Purple glass — ranging from almost black, to violet and pale amethyst — can also be found, as well as lustrous blues and greens. Red is very rare and collectable. When holding carnival glass to the light, colour changes can be observed as the base colour of the article is detected through the layers of the metallic surface sprays. Some carnival glass, such as that produced by the Imperial factory, had a gold or silver lustre finish, but this coloration is rare and expensive.

In England, the Sowerby factory made the new iridescent glass during the 1920s and 30s, under the tradenames 'Sunglow' (orange shades), and 'Rainbow Lustre' (blue or amethyst). The Crystal Glass Co in Australia produced carnival glass contemporaneously, as did various factories in Holland, Scandinavia and Czechoslovakia. In spite of this competition, however, the Americans appear to have retained their hold on the market.

A huge variety of everyday objects was made: bowls, dishes, plates, goblets, mugs, tumblers, decanters, water and punch sets, hatpins and holders, powder bowls, bottles, trinket pots, biscuit barrels, sugar and cream sets, and even beads.

The pressed patterns varied enormously, too, with the so-called 'Grape and Cable', both from Northwood and Fenton, and the 'Heavy Grape', from Imperial, being the best known.

Flower and fruit designs were popular and included 'Wild Rose', 'Raspberry', 'Daisy and Plume', 'Acorn Burrs', 'Three Fruits', 'Wishbone' (showing a pattern of orchids), and 'Fern', all by Northwood. The Fenton factory produced 'Wild Blackberry', 'Orange Tree', 'Captive Rose', 'Vintage' (showing grapes and leaves), 'Butterfly and Berry', 'Acorns', 'Autumn Acorns', 'Iris', 'Holly', 'Wreath of Roses', 'Birds and Cherries', 'Floral and Grape', and 'Dandelion'.

It is thought that the American

factories produced more than a thousand patterns and, apart from those mentioned above, geometric designs were also employed, as were scenes of windmills, houses and trees. Another frequently used design was that of a peacock or peacock's tail. Fenton brought out the 'Peacock and Urn' pattern, and this was copied by Millersburg, Northwood and Dugan. 'Peacock at the Fountain' was a variation on this theme created by Northwood, while 'Peacock and Grape' was devised by Fenton. Stylized peacocks' tails were used in the patterns 'Heart and Vine' (Fenton), 'Nippon' (Northwood) and 'Peacock Tail' (Fenton).

Carnival glass is priced according to the colour and rarity of the pressed design. The cheapest examples are those which feature the marigold 'Grape and Cable' pattern, and a shallow fruit dish in this style would cost from about £20–£25. The rarest colour is blue, regardless of pattern, and a good example in this colour would cost from about £40 upwards. Purple and dark green are also sought-after shades, and cost about £30 upwards for a shallow fruit dish.

CHAMBER POTS

☆ **BARGAIN BUY**
A Royal Winton chamber pot with colourful transfer printed design in blue, green and pink. £15

Chamber pots are generally used as plant holders by collectors today. Pottery examples with decorative patterns are in demand, especially those with blue and white transfer-printed scenes or elaborate floral motifs. Quite often, Victorian toilet and washstand sets included two chamber pots. These pairs are sought after, and one needs to be quick off the mark in buying them. In contrast, plain white pots may be purchased for as little as £3 or £4, and look most effective when containing a fern or other plant.

Some people collect chamber pots according to their manufacturers rather than their surface patterns, and examples by Minton, Wedgwood, Doulton, and Bishop and Stonier are popular today. A Bishop and Stonier chamber pot will sell for about £22–£25; a late Minton piece for about £40–£50; and a scenic 'blue and white' specimen from £30–£60 depending on the pattern.

At present, chamber pot collecting appears to have gone into something of a decline. Now is the time to buy as pieces will eventually come back into fashion and prices are likely to rise steeply.

CHARACTER JUGS

There is sometimes confusion between the terms 'Toby jug' and 'character jug'. The former consists of a seated male figure wearing a tricorn hat (which gives the jug its lip), holding a jug of ale in one hand balanced on his knee, and sometimes a pipe in the other (although numerous variations on this theme exist — see: *Toby Jugs*). The character jug, on the other hand, merely portrays the head and neck of a man or woman.

Amusing or grotesque heads and faces have decorated jugs since about 500 BC, and the practice has continued throughout the ages. In the Midlands, salt-glazed portrait jugs were made depicting historical figures such as Napoleon, Nelson, and the Duke of Wellington. The Martin brothers portrayed almost gargoyle-like faces on some of their jugs, and spirit flasks modelled by Leslie Harradine, of about 1909, featured famous politicians of the day. But it wasn't until the 1930s, when Royal Doulton (see: *Royal Doulton*) introduced their now-famous range of character jugs

John Barleycorn, designed by Charles Noke, issued from 1934–1960. £40–£45

— based on figures from English literature and history — that a whole new subject for collectors was born.

The first character jug was produced in 1934 portraying John Barleycorn, and this was an instant success. It was closely followed by models of Old Charley, Sairey Gamp, Parson Brown, and Dick Turpin. Since then, over 150 characters have appeared on these variously sized jugs ranging from large ones (5¼–7½ inches), to small (3½–4 inches), miniature (2¼–2½ inches), and tinies (1¼ inches). Not all the jugs have remained in production, and those withdrawn are obvious collector's pieces — being scarcer and more valuable than modern examples.

The most famous and collectable Doulton character jug is the Clown. Two versions were produced: the first, with orange hair, was made in 1937 and withdrawn in 1942; followed by the white-haired clown, introduced in 1951 and withdrawn in 1955. An orange-haired clown was sold at auction in 1985 for £1500 — an indication of how prices have escalated for the rarest pieces.

Sairey Gamp by Royal Doulton. £55

Dealers specializing in Royal Doulton character jugs know exactly which models are in or out of production, but those less knowledgeable in the field may have difficulty in identifying end-of-range pieces. The amateur collector would therefore find Richard Dennis's book *Doulton Character Jugs* most helpful, available at bookshops specializing in antiques.

Of the jugs still in production, one can still pay less for these at an antique fair, and even withdrawn models can be reasonably priced if you know where to look. The miniature jug of 'Arry and 'Arriet, the cockney costermongers, can be found for about £20, while an example depicting Sairey Gamp might be priced in the region of £50–£60.

CHEESE DISHES

Wedge-shaped cheese dishes can be found at most antique fairs, and the range of patterns and shapes offers enormous scope for collectors. In some examples, the angled surface was curved downwards, the handle scrolled, and the whole decorated by flowers. Others were of plain shape, and blue and white dishes of simple form (see: *Blue and White Transfer-Printed Ware*) look particularly attractive displayed on a white tablecloth or on a pine dresser. Victorian examples are favoured and usually cost from £30–£40.

A wedge-shaped Victorian cheese dish with hand-painted design in bright colours. £30

Cheese dishes from the 1920s and 30s are less ornate and more functional in shape, although 'cottage' ones (see: *Cottage Ware*) have a novelty value. Grimwades and Price Brothers are the best known for this kind of cheese dish. Carlton ware dishes (see: *Carlton Ware*) are pretty with their flowers in relief. Novelty cheese dishes were also made, and the model designed by Elizabeth Radford — in a plain semi-matt glaze — has a slice of cheese cut out from its lid. These amusing pieces can be purchased for about £16.

Domed Stilton dishes are expensive, and a Wedgwood example of dark blue jasperware, with white patterns in relief, is normally priced at over £100.

Prices vary according to size, surface patterning and condition. Always examine the stand, as quite often this is discoloured or stained, and cannot be bleached out. If wanted for domestic use, pieces with cracks and chips are best avoided. For the purpose of decoration, however, minor faults are acceptable and damaged pieces are often found at vastly reduced prices. They can be displayed in such a way that the fault is hidden.

C

CHINA CASED CLOCKS

Clocks have always been more than just functional, and have long been admired for their decorative value in the home — china-cased clocks fulfil this role, perhaps more than any other type. Many 19th century examples are beyond the reach of the average collector with prices for a 'Vienna' clock in excess of £1500, but some Victorian examples and those of later manufacture can be purchased reasonably.

The Victorians produced large florid clocks, which some collectors find over-ornate and garish. The cases for these can measure as much as 18 × 16 inches, modelled in the rococo style with hand-painted flowers. These are sometimes accompanied by side ornaments or garnitures, such as matching pair of vases, although many sets have been split up over the years. Due to their large size, these clocks are generally less expensive. A set consisting of a large clock decorated in green with gilt birds and foliage, and with matching tall vases, might sell for about £70–£80. The clock alone would probably cost £40–£50.

Smaller clocks were made in a variety of designs. Art Nouveau examples were adorned frequently with maidens on each side of the clock face, while Edwardian examples had transfer-printed portraits of young girls on the column below the dial. A 1930s example of cream-coloured china featured a coach and horses galloping across it, accompanied by two matching vases. The price for a similar set, and for typical Edwardian pieces, would be about £30.

Prices are based on the rarity and appeal of the clock case, rather than on its

A large Victorian clock in green and gilt with florid pink roses. £50

movement. As a result, clocks are often found re-conditioned, with new movements. This can confuse the beginner, as the brightness of brass around the dial might imply that the case is also new. But signs of wear are usually present underneath the clock, and with Victorian examples the glaze is frequently crazed at the back.

Cases are sometimes sold without a movement in them at all, and this reduces their price. But take care — new movements that fit exactly into the appropriate aperture are difficult to find, and as many antique examples are of 'non-standard' type, it can cost more than the clock is worth to have them replaced by a specialist repairer.

Very few cases bear a maker's mark, although Art Nouveau clocks stamped 'Shaw & Copestake Ltd', and dated 1925 can be found. The presence of this type of mark increases the price, and this example costs around £25. A similar piece, with side vases, might be priced from £40 upwards.

CHRISTENING GOWNS

Victorian examples are displayed at most antique fairs and are reasonably priced. There seems to have been a slump in the market recently, so now might be a good time to buy.

The gowns all follow the same style, with a yoke ruched at the breast, tiny puffed sleeves and a long skirt. But the fabric used, and the design on the skirt offer more variety.

Cotton gowns have pin-tucked panels, crochet inserts, and embroidery or lace insertions on the bodice, while the skirt

Cotton christening gown, the yoke and skirt made of broderie anglaise. £25–£30

was sometimes enhanced by cutwork, broderie anglaise, frills or lace. A few gowns have panelled insertions down the length of the skirt in lace, crochet or embroidered with flowers.

The dresses were mostly of white cotton, muslin or lawn, but one can find cream silk dresses with fine lace collars. Christening capes were made to match the latter, and these can also be found in fine cashmere, embroidered or fringed. Plain cotton gowns start at about £10, while those with added lace or embroidery sell for about £25. Silk examples are usually priced over £30.

Extremely finely made christening gowns may be found for purchase at antique markets and fairs, and are included frequently at specialist costume auctions.

CIGAR & CIGARETTE HOLDERS

Cigar and cigarette holders come in various materials and sizes. An Army and Navy Stores catalogue for 1907 offered 13 different sizes for cigar holders, and 20 sizes for cigarette holders. These were made in amber with hallmarked gold or silver rims, and also in horn, ivory, cherry wood, meerschaum, even paper and quill fitted with spiral tubes which could be adjusted to fit any cigar or cigarette. There was the 'Montgomery Moore' holder which had an absorbent cartridge, said to be the most effective anti-nicotine holder invented, and the 'Hygenic' cigarette holder which had a chamber filled with cotton wool, presumably to act as a filter. Mouthpieces were made of amber or quill.

Cased holders sometimes came 'complete with a 9-carat gold mount, best amber tube, quill mouthpieces, and long albatross stem for reading' (*sic*), but the majority were encased in leather or silver. They were oblong, or otherwise shaped to fit the holder. The silver cases invariably had a ring at one end for suspending on a watch chain.

Many fine holders and cases are found for purchase today, and are reasonably priced. An amber cigar holder with a silver rim costs about £10; if cased, the price would be nearer £15. Cigarette holders did not appear in plentiful supply before the 1920s, and usually cost a little more. Bakelite examples (uncased) can be found for about £10–£20.

Cigar and cigarette cases were made from *c*.1860 onwards of crocodile, lizard and elephant skin, pigskin, velvet, roan and Russian leather, and silver. They were oblong or square, and silver ones were sometimes curved to fit snugly into the back pocket. They were designed to carry either a single or double row of cigars or cigarettes.

Silver cases are highly collectable, and make an attractive display. Styles were either plain, sometimes with a monogram or initial, or elaborately scrolled and engraved with patterns of acanthus leaves and other decorations. Some were of hammered silver, or embossed with diagonal stripes and flowers. Prices for silver cases vary according to the pattern and weight of the case. A small plain case might cost as little as £15, but larger, more decorative cases range in price from £30–£100. Enamelled pieces, produced from *c*.1900–35, are among the most desirable and costly, and those with finely painted scenes in good condition can realize from £600–£1500 at auction. Erotic nudes and sporting subjects appear to be most popular with collectors.

Bakelite cigarette holder in case. £35

C

CIGARETTE CARDS

Churchman's Boy Scout series published in 1916. Single card £2, complete set of 50 will cost £100

These originated in America in the 1880s as spin-offs of trade cards, which had been used extensively in Europe. They were adopted in America by cigarette manufacturers and used as card stiffeners to protect the contents of the flimsy paper packets. Firms soon began using the stiffeners as a means of advertising, and with the new process of colour lithography (introduced in *c.*1880) they decorated their cards with a picture on one side and a list of products on the other. It is believed that Allen and Ginter were among the first to issue cigarette cards in Britain in 1884, followed in *c.*1887 by W. D. & H. O. Wills. Wills' first series in the late 1890s was entitled 'Advertising Cards (Serving Maid)' and a single card from this set is valued today at £400.

In 1897 the series 'Beauties, Collotype' was issued by the London tobacco firm Taddy, and cards from this set are sought after, now costing about £50 each. Other manufacturers followed suit, hoping to entice smokers with their variety of insert cards, and examples by Ainsworth of Harrogate, Alberge and Bromet of London, and MacDonald of Glasgow are all in demand.

There was great rivalry between British and American tobacco firms, particularly when the newly formed American Tobacco Company acquired the British firm of Ogdens. The British responded by amalgamating 13 companies to form the Imperial Tobacco Co in 1901. Present-day collectors benefit from the battle between the rival forces, as cigarette cards played an important part in wooing customers from one brand to another, attracted as they were by the increasing number of new series of cards produced by each company.

During the period 1894–1908 over 800 different cards were issued in Ogden's 'Guinea Gold' series. These were black and white photographs of actresses, famous personalities, politicians and sportsmen, and included also a wide variety of other topical subjects. Wills issued series such as 'Soldiers of the World', 'Cricketers', and 'Ships and Scouts'. The firm Players featured 'Country Seats and Arms', 'Badges and Flags of the British Regiments', and 'Ships' Figureheads' in their series. Gallahers produced sets of 'Actors and Actresses', 'Beauties', and 'English and Scottish Views'.

During World War I, when cigarette smoking increased enormously in popularity, military themes were favoured. New series included 'Recruiting Posters', 'Army Pictures', 'Cartoons etc', 'Arms and Armour', 'Army Ribbons and Buttons', and a whole host of other related topics.

Practically every subject was covered by the cigarette manufacturers: dogs, animals, clan tartans, statues and monuments, zoo studies, sports, flags, birds, sportsmen, lighthouses, trains, ships, the Royal Family, fish, film stars — the list is endless. This variety offers huge scope for the collector, and it can be difficult to know where to begin.

Some collectors prefer silk cards, while others concentrate on particular themes and subjects. The most popular category is sport, especially cricket, football and golf. Others collect ships, or cards related to the military, transport or cinema. Some collectors will only buy cards with butterflies or birds on them, regardless of the rest of the set.

Prices vary enormously. Early and rare cards, pre-1918, realize several hundred pounds at auction, but a single

Gallaher Ltd Boy Scout series (Green back) published in 1911. Single card 80p, complete set of 100 is £80

*Another from a Boy
Scout series, this time
by the Co-operative
Wholesale Society. A
single card will cost
£10, the set £250.
Published in 1912*

card of Carreras' 'Film and Stage
Beauties' (1939) costs only 12p, as does
any card from Wills' 'Zoo' series (1926).
These complete sets are priced at about
£5–£6 each. Indeed, the majority of cards
issued between 1920–39 cost from £2–£10
a set, and may be found in large numbers
due to their mass-production.

Cigarette cards should be purchased in
mint condition, preferably unmounted.
Albums with the cards stuck down are of
lesser value than unmounted sets. Avoid
creased or dog-eared examples, unless the
card is rare or of personal value. It can
probably be replaced at a later date.

Many books and magazines have
been written on the subject of cigarette
card collecting, and a price guide or
catalogue is an invaluable asset. For
further reading the following are
recommended: *Cigarette Cards and
Novelties* by Frank Doggett; and
*Collecting Cigarette Cards and other Trade
Card Issues* by Dorothy Bagnall.

CLAY PIPES

S moking began in the late-16th
century with the import of tobacco,
and the production of clay pipes
commenced shortly afterwards,
continuing until the 1930s. Early pipes
were largely undecorated, although a few
were adorned on the mouth of the bowl
and stem with simple motifs created by a
roulette wheel. The 1850s saw the
introduction of the 'churchwarden' pipe
which was almost three feet in length, but
these were impractical and were soon
phased out. The beautifully carved
meerschaum pipes of the Victorian era
competed with those of clay and, as a
result, manufacturers turned to making
'fancies' or 'fancy clays'. These portrayed

all manner of decorations. Pipes were made with bowls shaped like heads — sometimes featuring famous personalities such as the comedian Ally Soper, immediately recognizable with his grotesquely long nose. Portraits of negroes, jockeys and famous statesmen were also popular. The pipes were given a coat of varnish before baking in order to imitate meerschaum.

Some bowls had patterns in relief and showed acorns, leaves, ribbing, basketwork, fish scales, flowers, fruit, inn signs, animals and sporting pastimes.

Labourers favoured short pipes as they were lighter to hold between their teeth as they worked, for which purpose Scottish manufacturers created the 'cutty sark'. If the stem was too long, the owner could break it down to his liking.

Although clay pipes are easily damaged, many Victorian pieces have survived. Prices start from about £6 for a plain pipe, although decorative examples featuring footballers or other sporting subjects will cost from £25 in good condition. At a recent auction, a lot comprising about 15 pipes, some plain and all with slight damage on the stems, sold for only £12. In marked contrast, highly ornate meerschaum pipes of late 19th century date range in price from about £350 to over £2000.

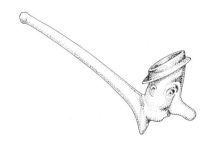

A pipe showing a caricature of the comedian Ally Soper. £25

CLIFF, CLARICE

Clarice Cliff (1900–70) was one of the most exciting designers of pottery during the late 1920s and 1930s, and her work is much sought after. She joined the Burslem firm of A. J. Wilkinson at the age of 17 and was encouraged to study design by Colley Shorter who, with his brother, had taken over Wilkinsons from their father. The brothers also acquired the Newport Pottery and in 1925 Clarice began designing the first of her 'Bizarre' pottery series. Adorned with coloured bands and diamond shapes in bold colours, the new range was a huge success. By 1930 Clarice had become Art Director of the company and continued to design new pottery shapes and decorative schemes in the Art Deco taste.

The 'Biarritz' range had rectangular plates, and covered sugar bowls in oblong shapes with curved bases and flat tops. 'Conical' was sharply angular in shape, the handles to the cups jutting out as solid triangles. 'Bonjour' was round, with teapots, cream and sugar sets echoing the circular theme, and the 'Stamford' design was reminiscent of cubism.

Colours were bright and exciting: ultramarine, vivid yellow and green. The 'Delicia' pattern of scarlet and orange poppies, with a red, blue, turquoise and

An earthenware cruet hand-painted in bright colours within a printed outline. £80–£100

purple streaked glaze, was used on the 'Stamford' shape.

Surface patterns were varied, ranging from the geometric to stark stylizations of trees and other forms in bold shades of black, cream, yellow and orange. In complete contrast, Clarice designed the 'My Garden' series, displaying more subdued pieces with flowers in relief ornamenting the handles or bases, perhaps with just a single spray across a vase. Her sense of fun is conveyed in her dancing figurines and wall masks (see: *Art Deco Face Masks*), while other novelties included book ends shaped like houses, pouter pigeon pipe holders, cheeky-faced fruit bowls, and ashtrays adorned with fashionable 1920s girls in spotted trousers.

Another well-known pattern was 'Crocus', introduced in the late 1930s and produced until the 1950s. This shows a fairly conventional line of crocus plants hand-painted in yellow and purple, above an orange base, used to decorate dinner and tea wares, vases, egg cups, cruets, jugs and bowls.

Pieces by Clarice Cliff have become increasingly sought after in recent years, and prices can be high. A two-person breakfast set in the 'Bonjour' shape may cost over a thousand pounds, but there are much cheaper items to be found. A conical cruet, brightly splashed with colour, can be found for about £25 to £30, and 'Crocus' pattern wares remain reasonably priced because of the quantity produced. A small (8 inches high) 'My Garden' vase can be found for about £30, and a bird pipe holder for £30–£40.

Vases and plates with bold colours and designs, for example in the 'Fantasque' pattern featuring stylized trees, are now fetching several hundred pounds at auction — purchased by both American and European collectors.

Honey pot of 'bizarre' design decorated in vivid colours on beige ground. £40–£50

CLOCKWORK & TINPLATE TOYS

E arly clockwork toys have now become so collectable — a Lehmann or Bing toy will cost anything from £300 to thousands of pounds — that beginners are advised to purchase examples from the 1930s. Good clockwork and tinplate toys were made during this period and many pieces are modestly priced. Unmarked examples are always cheaper and a wind-up motor cyclist with goggled rider was sold recently for only £10 at auction. Triang Minic vehicles are collectable and come with or without clockwork motors. Hornby train sets in various gauges are also worth looking out for, and can be found reasonably priced. A railway set with two engines (one damaged), a small amount of rolling stock, a tinplate station with a background of rolling hills, and track was recently on sale at an antique fair for only £85. A Hornby crane in good condition was priced at £25.

Aeroplanes are also inexpensive, and can be found for about £40. Look out for Meccano sets. Although not tinplate, they are worth collecting. Complete boxed sets

Selection of post-war tin toys from £25 upwards

have achieved astronomical prices, but Set No. 10, for example, will cost about £100.

Mickey Mouse and other cartoon characters are highly prized and the collector should purchase these if reasonably priced. Ships and boats are scarce, possibly due to rust after immersion in water, and moderately priced examples are also worth considering.

It is important to check the condition of the paintwork, and scratched and dented pieces are best avoided. Ensure, also, that the clockwork motor operates satisfactorily. Articles accompanied by their original boxes generally fetch higher prices. Ideal hunting grounds are jumble sales and flea markets.

COFFEE CANS

This is one of the widest areas for collectors, along with that of tea cups and saucers (see: *Cups and Saucers*), and the range of factories, patterns and dates appears unlimited.

Coffee cans are small straight-sided cups (like mugs) and, for collectors, can also include the *demi-tasse* (half cup) shape which is smaller. Coffee cans usually measure up to 2¾ inches in height, while *demi-tasse* cups can be as little as 2 inches high. Coffee cans became popular in the 18th century and many French examples were made as individual items, and not part of a set. Later, finely painted cups were made as cabinet pieces, not intended for use. The factories of Sèvres in France, and Derby in England were fine exponents of these.

Antique fairs and flea markets usually have a broad selection of pieces. Collectors often purchase coffee cans without saucers and, in fact, many were made as part of a trio consisting also of a tea cup, and a saucer which served both vessels. Dealers in flea markets often underprice cans, in the belief that they are lacking their saucers.

Coffee cans of Derby and Worcester manufacture command the highest prices, especially early pieces from the late 18th and early 19th centuries. These are likely to cost in the region of £80 each. Early patterns were composed frequently of simple hand-painted flowers, with pale pink roses featuring strongly, especially in the Worcester range. Later Worcester cups with paintings by James Stinton are highly collectable and will cost £70–£80 each. Derby patterns in dark blue, orange and gold are also in demand — antique examples cost about £70, but later pieces dating from the 1930s, in similar styles, vary between £35 and £50. Other 19th century manufacturers popular with collectors include Minton, Spode, Davenport, Mason, Newhall and Wedgwood.

'Blue and white' coffee cans from the Victorian and Edwardian eras (see: *Blue and White Transfer-Printed Ware*) have an appeal all their own, and prices can be surprisingly modest — starting from £10 for Copeland Spode's 'Italian' design, or a delicately patterned can from Royal Crown Derby. Many 'blue and white' pieces were not marked, and are cheaper than those bearing a backstamp. A varied collection of undocumented pieces can be built up for little outlay.

During the 20th century, fine china cans and cups continued to be made. Factories such as Aynsley, Crown Staffordshire, Tuscan, Paragon and Royal Albert all produced attractive examples, priced today at about £15 each. Bell China manufactured some charming cups and these are still under-rated, costing about £7 or £8.

A Flight, Barr and Barr Worcester coffee can, showing typical handle. £60

Noritaké china from Japan remains relatively inexpensive, although prices are expected to rise with growing demand (see: *Noritaké China*). Noritake produced a huge variety of patterns, from the scenic 'Tree in the Meadow' series, to the classic 'White and Gold' styles. Heavily gilded and ornate *demi-tasse* cups and saucers were also made, with jewel-like colours. Prices are around £18–£25 for a cup and saucer, although an ornate example in green and silver was bought recently for only £7.

COMMEMORATIVE GLASS

Victorian pressed glass of a commemorative nature (see: *Press-Moulded Glass*) was manufactured cheaply and is in plentiful supply. Earlier pieces of hand-engraved or etched glass have become increasingly expensive in recent years, so for the collector of modest . means the mass-produced wares of the 19th century merit consideration.

Commemorative plate in amber pressed glass celebrating Victoria's Golden Jubilee. £20–£25

Industrial achievements were popular commemorative subjects in the mid-1800s, evidenced, for example, by a press-moulded tankard which was made to celebrate the construction of a high-level bridge at Newcastle upon Tyne in 1850. Famous people and events were also portrayed. Frosted glass busts of statesmen such as Disraeli and Gladstone were produced, and the death of General Gordon in 1885 was commemorated on the surfaces of glass wares. Allegorical figures such as Punch and Judy, John Bull, and Britannia were used in addition.

Victoria's long reign supported a prolific souvenir industry and numerous wares such as plates and sugar bowls were adorned with her portrait. A Golden

Jubilee plate was produced by Sowerby's in 1887 depicting the Queen. They later reproduced the plate for the Diamond Jubilee, with only the wording and date changed.

Commemorative plates were usually of clear glass, although sometimes coloured brown or amber, and sell for £20–£30 each depending on the pattern. Greener's made fine examples showing the monarch's crown with a crossed orb and sceptre, and these are priced at about £60.

Pieces bearing a maker's stamp are dearer than unmarked specimens. A sugar bowl of anonymous manufacture, commemorating the Golden Jubilee, was bought recently for only £7, although similar articles have been seen at antique fairs for £12–£14.

COMMEMORATIVE WARE

Blue and white transfer-printed mug made by Wedgwood & Co (Tunstall) for the coronation of George VI. £25–£30

Mugs and other wares commemorating royalty were produced in vast numbers during the late 19th century, and these represent a good starting point for the novice collector as there is a wide choice and variety available. Victoria's long reign gave the souvenir industry a boost, although there are few examples to be found commemorating her coronation, and a Swansea mug celebrating this event will fetch about £800 today.

The weddings of Victoria's eldest children, the Prince of Wales (later Edward VII) and the Princess Royal were both commemorated in pottery and porcelain. Victoria's Golden Jubilee in 1887, and the Diamond Jubilee in 1897 resulted in a vast number of items being made. Golden Jubilee mugs were decorated with a monochrome transfer, although some were further embellished by hand-painting. By the time of the Diamond Jubilee, production methods had improved and the colours were bright and varied. A fine example commemorating this event will cost about £50.

Coronations have always featured on souvenir wares, and the mug produced when George V was crowned in 1911 is today priced at about £50. The mug made to mark his marriage in 1893 is rarer and costlier — about £80 for a specimen in fine condition.

Coronation commemoratives made for Edward VIII (the Duke of Windsor) are not expensive and can be found for £20 upwards. Examples bearing the words 'Abdicated December 10th 1936', presumably added to help sell surplus stock, are rare and more desirable, and as such command correspondingly higher prices.

Most popular with collectors interested in monarchs are wares decorated with portraits of Edward VII, Queen Alexandra and Queen Elizabeth II. However, very little was produced in the way of souvenirs for the present Queen's marriage to Prince Philip.

Fine quality items do not necessarily command the highest prices. Some of the smaller factories were restricted in their output, and their wares are scarce and sometimes expensive. This is evidenced, for example, by a mug seen recently on display at an antique fair, adorned with a black and white transfer-print commemorating the divorce of Princess Margaret. The dealer was asking £400 for it — an enormous price, but indicative of how rare pieces are valued.

Modern commemoratives are also worth collecting. Again, it is not necessarily quality that will appreciate,

China mug by Hammersley to commemorate Victoria's Diamond Jubilee. £50–£60

but lack of quantity.

The collector should beware of imitations, since reproduction mugs and beakers are beginning to appear on the market. For this reason, it is important to inspect the underside of a mug for signs of wear. Reproductions have a clean white base, and the over-all glaze is shiny.

COOPER, SUSIE

Susie Cooper's china and pottery has been appreciated by the public for over 60 years. She began her career as a designer with A. E. Gray and Co in 1922 and became Art Director of the firm a few years later. Her designs for china were so successful that Gray's awarded her a personal backstamp showing a stylized steamer within a square, with the words 'Hand-painted. Gray's Pottery, Hanley, England. Designed by Susie Cooper'.

Cooper's early work followed the fashions of the 1920s, displaying bright colours, especially yellow and orange, and banded and geometric patterns. (See also *Cliff, Clarice*.) Flowers and fruit motifs figured largely, too. 'The 'Gloria Lustre' range made its appearance at about this time (see: *Lustre Ware*) and although most pieces do not bear Cooper's name, the backstamp with its radiant sun in black or gold can be safely attributed to her. The lustre pieces are seldom seen today, and cost £70 upwards.

In 1930 Susie Cooper left Gray's and opened her own workshop at the Chelsea Works, Burslem. Her backstamp for this period consists of a black triangle with the words 'A Susie Cooper Production'. This was later replaced by a stylized signature and 'Crown Works, Burslem, England'. From 1932–1939, a leaping deer symbol was used. It was during this

An Art Deco cup and saucer from a set of four, the stylized pattern in bright colours. £35

period that the shapes 'Kestrel', patterned with varying bands of colour, and 'Curlew', bearing stylized curved lines, were made.

The dots and dashes that were to become so characteristic of her work were introduced in 1932, and 'Polka Dot' in blue, red and orange was a huge success. Lithographic designs were employed from about 1935, and were so precisely executed that they were mistaken for hand-painting. 'Dresden Spray' on the Kestrel shape shows a delicate arrangement of pink, purple and yellow flowers against a plain ground, although the 'Briar Rose' pattern is most frequently seen at antique fairs. It is important to examine these wares carefully, and to look for signs of age, as production continued up until 1963. A teaset in 'Briar Rose' of an early date will cost over a hundred pounds, but plates, cups and saucers can be bought for about £18 each.

Look out for the more unusual pieces, such as the studio items which appear in many different styles. The 'sgraffito' wares also merit attention with their designs 'scratched' into the clay. These can be found for about £20–£40 each, but occasionally one will have to pay more.

Pieces produced during the 1950s are now collectable, and represent an area worth concentrating on. A bone china coffee set with a delicate pattern of tiny stars and a coloured interior of rust or pale blue can be bought for £40–£60. A late 1950s set with a wide straight-sided coffee pot and matching cups, decorated with black and white fruit, each having a different coloured interior, was purchased recently for only £15 — a rare bargain and one sure to appreciate in value. The studio wares, neglected for too long by collectors, are now beginning to make an impact and prices are expected to rise.

COPPER KETTLES

Copper kettles in traditional shapes will cost anything up to £70 or £80, according to their age and condition. They are popular additions to households with open fireplaces, where they can be effectively displayed on the hearth. Some have handles of wrought iron, turned ebony or wood, and occasionally bakelite was used on late Victorian kettles (see: *Bakelite*).

It is important to check the base, handle and seams of a copper kettle as these areas provide clues to age and condition. Many modern reproduction kettles are distressed in an effort to make them look old, and the dents and slight blackening of the copper can be most effective. But the seams and rivets cannot be aged, so these are the areas in which to begin your examination.

Kettles come in all sizes, as stated in an Army and Navy catalogue at the turn of the century which offered tea kettles in copper and wrought iron ranging from one pint to an amazing 20-pint capacity. There were bachelor kettles which were wide bottomed, square gas stove kettles with a copper body and tin top, and spirit kettles which stood on a stand over a small spirit lamp. The latter were available in silver plate, brass or copper. The spirit kettle was supported on two lugs, and when boiled was tipped forward to fill the teapot.

Examples of spirit kettles are not often seen today, and as such command high prices — usually well over a hundred pounds.

More modestly priced are the early electric copper kettles, which can be found for £15–£20.

A copper kettle circa 1900. £50

C

CORKSCREWS

The basic principle of the corkscrew has changed little over the years, being composed of a spiral helix, fluted to give it strength, and attached to a handle or grip. Only slight modifications in the design and materials used have been implemented in the course of time, with a few innovations to make the drawing of the cork easier for the user.

The first corkscrews had simple horizontal grips, giving a T-bar effect and were made of nickel-plated or bronzed steel, silver, iron, wood or covered in leather. The wooden grips were turned, displaying all manner of grooved patterns, and sometimes had a small bristle brush at one end for cleaning the neck of the bottle. Simple examples will cost £6 or £8. Horn-handled corkscrews became popular as souvenirs, and had plated or silver end pieces. These sell from £10 upwards in good condition. In contrast, ornate silver examples of 18th-century manufacture, can realize over £400 at auction.

Metal corkscrews were available in a variety of shapes: bow screws had an oval ring of metal for a handle; eyebrow screws were so-called because the oval ring sprouted a wing of metal either side;

Selection of corkscrews from the Victorian period. £5–£15

Folding corkscrew in steel combined with a buttonhook. £5–£7

and folding corkscrews, sometimes called stirrup corkscrews, had a triangular handle into which the screw folded.

Champagne corkscrews had a spike at one end of the handle, presumably for breaking the wire that held the cork. The helix also took a different form and resembled the Archimedes screw, similar to a wooden screw. Pocket corkscrews came complete with an outer case of steel, nickel or silver, while travelling corkscrews, known also as peg and worm screws (because the handle was detachable and slotted into a hole at the top of the screw) could be found with handles of embossed silver and mother-of-pearl. Other travelling corkscrews were produced in conjunction with toilet sets, designed for opening bottles of medicine or toilet water. They were small and delicately made with handles that matched the accompanying buttonhooks (see: *Buttonhooks*) in mother-of-pearl, ivory, bone, or silver.

Some corkscrews were made of wire. Being of light construction they did not last long, and examples are scarce. Some were sold with patent medicines and consisted of a simple ring of wire with a short screw.

Mechanical corkscrews came on the scene in about 1880. Heeley & Son patented the A1 Double Lever which operated on a series of linked levers. The 'London Rack' by Lund, one of the most prolific inventors in the field, used the rack and pinion method, while other firms brought out versions of the double screw and wingnut corkscrew. Unmarked versions sell for between £20–£30.

Some corkscrews were spring loaded, and a few types used the 'lazy tongs' lever method, but these are hard to find and will cost as much as £50 or more.

Bottle openers were made for the Codd mineral water bottle (see: *Bottles —*

Glass), when customers were issued with a wooden plunger for releasing the marble seal. When crimped metal caps were invented, the crown bottle opener appeared. The first examples consisted of simple flattened rings of iron or steel with a shaft stamped with the maker's name. But later, novelty pieces were designed in the form of guitars, bottles, birds, figures, and even coffee pots. Other bottle openers operated on the 'hook' principle, when a metal projection was placed on the underside of the crown cap which could then be eased off by leverage. These range in price from £5–£8 for simple examples, and up to £50 for novelties.

CORNISH WARE

This blue and white striped domestic pottery was produced by T. G. Green of Derbyshire in the 1930s. Specific containers for culinary use, such as sugar and flour jars, had not been made in ceramics until then, and the Cornish ware was immediately popular.

This type of ware is vastly under-rated by collectors, and it is possible to buy pieces for as little as £2 or £3 at a flea market or jumble sale. Prices at antique fairs are higher, where a pint milk jug might cost £8–£9, and a lidded flour container £10–£12.

All manner of items were made for the kitchen: milk jugs; lidded sugar and flour jars; cups shaped like mugs with matching saucers; cruets and vinegar bottles; cream jugs; sugar basins; plates; coffee and teapots; and egg cups.

The ware is recognizable by its wide bands of blue and white, with a broader band of blue near the top of the article. The name 'Cornish Kitchen Ware' is marked underneath, enclosed in a striped

Left: Storage jar for flour (£8) and (right) matching coffee pot (£12)

shield, with the words 'T.G. Green. Made In England' printed in a ribbon-like banner above.

Another style of blue and white banded ware was made by the Paramount Pottery, and called 'Chef Ware'. Their mark consists of a man wearing a chef's hat in the centre of the lettering, placed underneath the article. These later pieces were produced from about 1946 to 1958, and should not be confused with Cornish ware. 'Chef Ware' is distinctive since the bands of colour are not equidistant, the white stripe being the broader, ending in white at the top of the item.

COTTAGE CLOCKS

A sharp Gothic version of the plain cottage clock, with a painted tablet. £65

These are basically smaller versions of the ogee clock (see: *American Ogee Clocks*) and were designed for the mantel shelf. The ogee moulding was dispensed with but the rectangular dial remained as did the glass-fronted door. Sometimes the painted tablet was replaced by a mirror. Cottage clocks were usually 7½–8½ inches high and were made in increasing numbers as skill in producing cheap steel springs developed. They were also a lightweight alternative to the heavier ogee clock.

Used as simple striking timepieces and alarm clocks, they never chime. German imitations of the American clock, which appeared at roughly the same period, are difficult to distinguish, but the maker's label which was pasted behind the pendulum will reveal the country of origin. American makers are Seth Thomas, Jerome and Company, Waterbury, Gilbert, and E. N. Welch. German manufacturers include Union Clock Company, Junghans, and Philipp Haas.

Prices start at around £25 for a simple non-striking timepiece, with an early alarm costing about £60.

Check that the maker's label or paper is pasted into the case, and that it is original and in good order. Reproduction labels are now available and can be substituted for the damaged original.

COTTAGE WARE

The idea of making ceramic items in the shape of cottages has been popular since the early 19th century, and several firms produced them. Regency and Victorian examples can cost several hundred pounds, but those made during the 1930s remain inexpensive. Carlton Ware (see: *Carlton Ware*) made biscuit barrels and cheese dishes in the shape of houses, with simple glazing over the smooth surfaces. The two most prolific producers of the period, however, were the Price Brothers and Grimwades.

Price's pottery cottages appear in varying shades of yellow, brown and cream, and were intended for use as cheese dishes, cruets, biscuit barrels, teapots, cream jugs and sugar basins, designed in matching sets. Prices range

Cottage style china by Grimwades. The teapot will cost £35–£40, the cruets about £15–£20 the pair, and the jam pots on its stand about £18–£22

from about £12 for a pair of cruets, to £18 for a cheese dish. The collector should examine pieces for signs of age and wear, as similar pottery is still being produced by the Price factory.

Grimwades created many cottage styles, with their decorative exteriors disguising the functional aspects of the piece. One of Grimwades' teapots in the form of a cottage displays a pink roof, tiny blue windows, and rambling roses around the door, with a water wheel on the reverse side. The teapot is stamped 'Grimwades. Ye Olde Mill. Hand Painted'.

Another cottage-type issued by Grimwades, under their 'Rubian Art' backstamp, is modelled as a Tudor cottage with well-defined black timbers under a shaded pink and yellow roof, with trees growing at the side.

A third style, under the trademark of 'Royal Winton', is of a cottage painted in more delicate colours, the roof shaded yellow and green, and the timbers less well defined. Hollyhocks adorn the base of the item.

Prices have escalated in recent years, and a sugar caster bought two years ago for £5 now costs between £15–£18. A teapot in any of the above-mentioned styles is usually priced from £30–£40, although smaller items in the 'Rubian Art' series are cheaper than those bearing the 'Royal Winton' backstamp. Wall plates vary in price between £14 and £28, and cruets are about £12–£15 a pair.

CRANBERRY GLASS

Cranberry glass came into vogue in Britain during the early Victorian era and is identifiable by its pinky red colour, reminiscent of runny strawberry jam. It is sometimes described incorrectly as 'ruby' glass, the latter being of a darker red colour — almost inky in appearance — and produced in Bohemia.

Red, in glass, is obtained by adding various metal oxides, such as gold, copper, iron, or manganese, or a combination of these to achieve pale and dark shades.

Clear glass was popular in England during the 18th century, although from *c.*1760 coloured lead glass was manufactured by factories in the Bristol area and the West Midlands. Shades of rich blue, yellow, deep green and amethyst were created. By the mid-1800s, cranberry glass was being made in large quantities in the Midlands, the home of pressed glass (see: *Press-Moulded Glass*). Although several cranberry pieces are distinctive for their fine quality, initial productions were intended for simple domestic use, or as seaside souvenirs and prizes at fairs. Typical examples were adorned with frilled edges and/or applied clear glass decorations. Small cranberry glass baskets had clear handles, and sugar bowls and cream jugs featured chain-work ornamentation and stood on feet that were pinched out in a leaf-type fashion.

Victorian shade with frilled edge in cranberry glass. £40–£60

Two cranberry wine glasses with clear stems. £20 each

Some cranberry wares were adorned additionally with vaseline and other coloured glass motifs (see: *Vaseline Glass*) to give an effect of contrast which is most attractive.

All manner of objects were made: large jugs with white enamelling, small sweetmeat dishes, sugar casters, baskets, vases, bells, lampshades, épergnes, custard cups, tumblers, pocket watch stands — the list is endless. Arranged against a window, or with a light shining from behind, cranberry glass will make a spectacular display.

Prices vary enormously. An ornate cranberry glass épergne with four or five fluted trumpets and hanging baskets can cost over £300, while many smaller items are more moderately priced. A cream jug with matching sugar bowl can be found for about £40; and a custard cup of simple design might be purchased for as little as £15. In view of its immense popularity, however, careful searching is needed to find items which are sensibly priced. It should also be noted that cranberry tablewares, in 19th century styles, are being reproduced today in England and Czechoslovakia — and sold through fine department stores.

CRESTED CHINA

Goss copy of the Orkney Craisie with the Derby coat of arms. £20–£25

This souvenir china was produced from *c.*1870–1935. The first manufacturer was W. H. Goss of Stoke-upon-Trent who made a fine glazed parian body (see: *Parian & Bisque*) for his wares. Each piece was marked with the heraldic arms of the town in which it was sold. The idea caught on, and soon other factories began to copy Goss's crested wares. The principal makers were Shelley, Carlton, Willow Art, and Arcadian, closely followed by Grafton and Savoy. These pieces were all clearly marked underneath with the factory's backstamp, Goss using the goshawk as his emblem. The Goss factory created their last piece in 1929, but other manufacturers carried on until the mid-30s.

Goss produced over 1500 different shapes adorned with more than 7000 styles of decoration, so the opportunity for collectors is enormous, especially as other factories were also producing different designs. Mugs, plates, beakers, cups and saucers were made, although of most interest to collectors are: the animals (£4–£10); busts and figures of famous people (£30–£80); buildings and monuments (£10–£25); clocks (£5–£15); hats (£5–£30); militaria subjects (£8–£15); monoplanes (£30–£50); seaside souvenirs (£4–£10); submarines and other ships (£10–£60); tanks (£8–£15); and transport themes (£10–£50).

Rare and unusual items to look out for include: the Arcadian Black Cat series (£30–£50); tanks by Carlton such as the 'Creme de Menthe' (£25), and the WWI tank with the crest of Shoreham on Sea (over £500); biplanes (£75); Goss's Rock of Gibraltar (£300); and St Ives Cross (£165).

Condition is important, and any chips or cracks will affect the price dramatically. Rare and unusual pieces command the highest prices (such as Carlton's WWI tank above) but if damaged their values may be reduced by half.

Unmarked pieces are always cheaper and not so highly sought after.

As there are so many items from which to choose, a price guide to the subject is invaluable — such as Nicholas Pine's *The Price Guide to Crested China* (available from Milestone Publications, Horndean, Hants).

Small crested jug showing the Bradford coat of arms. £6–£8

C

Crown Devon rose bowl with pastel-coloured flowers on soft beige background. £22–£25

Crown Devon ware washstand sets reach over £100

CROWN DEVON WARE

This pottery was made by S. Fielding & Co in Staffordshire and is extremely collectable.

The traditional patterns were nearly always placed on a beige background, finely painted in soft browns, pinks, blues and greens. Designs followed the flowing stylized patterns of Art Nouveau. The outlines were finely drawn, with a small amount of colour used to emphasize the decoration (see illustration). Washstand sets were made, priced today at about £120, as well as jugs, bread plates (see:

Bread Boards and Accessories), vases and all manner of domestic items. A bread plate costs about £18, and a pair of well-patterned vases sell for about £40–£60.

Crown Devon pottery of the 1930s is rapidly becoming collectable. This pretty 'cottage' earthenware is adorned characteristically with a background of green or yellow in a style similar to crazy paving, and with applied flowers in orange, pink and blue. Straight-sided spill vases were made, as were cruets, toast racks and other small items. Prices for these start from around £12 for a three-piece cruet on a stand, to £14 for a small toast rack.

CRUETS

S ilver cruets have become increasingly
expensive, but imitations in silver-
plate are both attractive and reasonably
priced. Most sought after are the cruets
on stands, which were popular in
Victorian and Edwardian times. These
consist of a tray-like base fitted with
apertures for the various glass bottles and
jars, surmounted by a central carrying
handle. The majority were equipped with
bottles for oil, vinegar and sauce,
accompanied by salt, pepper and mustard
containers. The designs found on silver-
plated examples are sometimes ornate,
with embossing or etching on the tray and
carrying handle. Prices for a complete set,
in good condition, start from about £60 or
£70. It is important to check that the
surface plating is intact, and that the
bottles all match and retain their original
stoppers. The glass should also be
examined for damage since the bases of
stoppers, and the corners of square
containers, are vulnerable and easily
chipped.

Glass cruets, complete with a
matching tray, are most attractive and are
usually found in hand-cut or pressed
styles (see: *Press Moulded Glass*). The
sharply faceted patterns of the former
catch and reflect the light, creating an
added brilliance. As above, examples
should always be inspected carefully for
damage, particularly on the stoppers and
bases. Finely-cut glass cruet sets for oil
and vinegar, salt, pepper and mustard will
cost from £20–£70; pressed examples
range from £10–£15.

Cruets were also made in porcelain
and pottery, and appear with great
variety. Carlton (see: *Carlton Ware*)
produced novelty pieces shaped like
tomatoes or flowers (about £14); Clarice

*Victorian cruet, the
gilding slightly worn.
£8*

89

Carlton Ware condiment set circa 1940, based on leaf design. £12–£15

Cliff (see: *Cliff, Clarice*) designed conical salt and pepper holders in bright Art Deco patterns (£25–£30 each); Grimwades (see: *Cottage Ware*) disguised the functional aspects of cruets under cottages (£10–£12); Crown Devon (see: *Crown Devon Ware*) produced pottery examples decorated with tiny flowers (£15 the set); and Elizabeth Radford (see: *Radford, Elizabeth*) designed softly-painted containers in rounded shapes (about £7–£8 for a pair).

Cruets shaped like tigers, fish, birds, and in other novel forms, were also imported into England. Occasionally, these may be found for purchase for under £5.

CUPS & SAUCERS

A wide and representative collection of 19th and early 20th century styles can be built up for very little outlay although early cups and saucers are expensive (see: *Coffee Cans*). An example with Copeland Spode's 'Italian' pattern in blue and white (see: *Blue and White Transfer-Printed Ware*) costs about £12, while Booth's 'Real Olde Willow' pieces (see: *Willow Patterned Ware*) are a little more expensive at £15. Since this design is still being made, the collector should look out for cups and saucers with gilded decorations, bearing the old mark underneath. Royal Crown Derby cups with exquisite floral patterns are dearer at about £30, and their backstamps should also be examined to ensure that they are not of modern manufacture.

A wide range of imaginative designs was produced in the 1920s–30s, inspired by Art Deco stylizations. Shelley produced angular-shaped cups and saucers with bold triangular handles, and these are priced from about £15–£20. Pieces with floral motifs and woodland scenes cost about £9–£12, and are of a more traditional shape. Carlton (see: *Carlton Ware*) made cups in primrose and foxglove patterns which sell for about £10–£15. Aynsley China sets cost about £8, although a rare example with a hand-painted butterfly on the handle was found recently for about £20.

Other factory names to look out for are Hammersley; Paragon (fast becoming collectable); Royal Albion, who produced beautifully patterned china in the Edwardian style; Royal Albert; Tuscan; Crown Staffordshire; and Bell China.

Art Deco cup and saucer (centre) £10. The two others are by Clarice Cliff and will cost £20–£30 each

DECANTERS & STOPPERS

For those on a limited budget, it is best to concentrate on decanters of late 19th and early 20th century manufacture as the prices for these have remained reasonable.

Decanters come in various shapes according to the wine or spirit they were designed to contain. There are square and bottle-shaped ones, 'onion' decanters with a round base and long neck, and ships' decanters with their wide flat bases made for stability on rough seas. Prices for these vary according to the design, the amount of hand cutting on the decanter, and the condition in which it is found.

Spirit decanters, with their heavy glass stoppers (see illustration), are usually straight-sided with squared off corners, although the type known as 'Old Dutch' has indentations on each side forming a column at the four corners. Some decanters have silver collars and these, and heavily-cut examples, usually cost from £60–£80. 'Onion' decanters (see illustration) were either plain, diamond cut, or had 'thumb print' indentations, sometimes with fluted rims at the neck which were finely etched. These range in price between £25 and £40. Ships' decanters cost from £40–£60, and their elegant shapes are popular with collectors.

Miniature decanters were also produced in the 19th century, and can sometimes be found for as little as £15 for a nicely-cut example. Many were intended originally as oil and vinegar bottles for cruet sets (see: *Cruets*), or were traveller's samples.

The majority of antique decanters no

Heavy cut glass Victorian spirit decanter with ornate stopper. £80

longer retain their original stoppers, and have been re-fitted with other contemporary ones in keeping with the style of the piece.

The absence of the original stopper does not necessarily reduce the price, except in the case of coloured and/or ornate decanters where the 'marriage' is evident.

Stoppers are also collectable and there exist an enormous variety including: mushroom shapes, and those of round, bull's eye, lozenge and spire form. These cost from about £2 upwards, although examples of coloured glass will be slightly more.

It is important to examine decanters carefully. Stoppers are found frequently with chips at the base, and the necks and rims of decanters are vulnerable and subject to damage. Heavily cut decanters should also be inspected for chips as these can be lost in the complexity of the pattern and overlooked. Small and insignificant chips can be ground down by a specialist repairer, but cracks cannot be mended.

Late Victorian sherry decanter in cut glass 'onion' shape. £45–£50

DINKY TOYS & OTHERS

P re-war models of Dinky toys are not as collectable as later ones. This is because later examples have not suffered from the metal fatigue that causes so many early models to literally crumble away. Boxed Dinky toys in pristine condition command high prices and some will be as much as three or four hundred pounds each. For the beginner, however, more modestly priced models can be found, such as cars and small vans bearing advertisements. These usually cost about £60–£80, while Ferrari saloons

94

Jaguar XK140. Issued in 1956. About £50. The articulated Bedford lorry was issued first in 1948, then re-issued twice more, so had a long production life. £30–£50

are slightly cheaper at about £50 each.

Lesney models offer more scope for the collector and bargains can be found on junk stalls and at jumble sales. Again, look out for advertising models, or cars no longer in production. Tractors and agricultural toys have been largely neglected, and would make a good starting point to a collection. Prices begin at about £10 upwards.

DOLL'S HOUSE FURNITURE

Doll's houses and their contents give an insight into how our ancestors lived. The tiny pieces of furniture were replicas of those owned by contemporary householders. One only has to look inside a Georgian 'baby house', as it was known, to note the shelves of tiny pewter plates in the kitchen, and catch a glimpse of a life that has vanished.

Victorian doll's houses, like those of their real life counterparts, were crammed full of possessions. The kitchen had its dresser packed with plates, with miniature tin jugs hung from hooks, a pine table, and a cooking range; the drawing room was usually furnished with a *chaise-longue*, an overstuffed armchair, pictures, clocks, vases and ornaments of every description, even tiny busts on pedestals. Nothing was left out. In the 1930s doll's houses had angular furniture in the Art Deco style, and even accessories such as telephones, crystal sets and radios were included.

All types of furniture and goods were copied. Minute Bentwood chairs can be found, as well as padded seated dining chairs, and ornate gilt chairs on spindly legs. Miniature glass was made from around 1840 and mostly came from Bohemia (now Czechoslovakia) or Lauscha in Thuringia (Germany).

The first English doll's house appeared around 1700, as an adult amusement rather than a child's plaything. Miniature furniture was sometimes adorned with gold or silver filigree, and cabinets were made in wood, always correct in every tiny detail. Wooden German tablewares with painted sprays of flowers were popular in the mid-1800s, and ivory, too, was used. Displays of food for the table were made from gesso or plaster of Paris, and painted in realistic colours. Pressed tinplate was used as early as the mid-18th

Wickerwork miniature furniture. £12 upwards each piece

D

century, mainly in America, but this material is more commonly associated with the 1920s and 30s when minute replicas of gas cookers appeared. Plastic and bakelite became popular for the mass market and a variety of doll's house items were made in these materials.

Not all doll's house furniture was professionally made. Fathers laboured for beloved daughters, creating dining chairs from ingeniously folded wire wound round with wool. Standard lamps were made from cotton reel bases and pleated paper shades, while sea shells did duty for almost every kind of utensil. The houses themselves were painstakingly concocted from wooden orange boxes during the 1930s and 40s, not cardboard as now. Pictures fashioned from postage stamps adorned the walls, and tiny mirrors were made from silver foil. Corks, bottle tops, wooden toothpicks, scraps of wallpaper, and carpet leftovers — all were employed imaginatively by the enthusiastic amateur.

Specialist antique shops have the choicest pieces, with a range of furniture intricately carved and superbly upholstered in mahogany and other fine woods. More modest items, however, can be found at antique fairs, junk shops and jumble sales. Half the fun is in the search.

Silver filigree and ornate wooden furniture of the 19th century is best left to the serious collector as prices are high. Later examples offer more scope, such as the pressed tin-plate of the 1920s and 30s, and the early plastic of the 1940s. Such items can be bought for a few pounds. Porcelain bathroom fittings might cost around £10 each, but simple wooden settees, sideboards, and the like can be found for as little as £3–£4. Condition is very important, and damaged miniatures are reflected by correspondingly lower prices.

DRESSING TABLE SETS

The most desirable — and expensive — sets are those of hallmarked silver, dating from the Victorian and Edwardian eras. Examples were frequently heavily embossed with swirling leaves, flowers and other decorative motifs, and consisted of a hand mirror, hair brush, clothes brush, comb, matching buttonhooks (see: *Buttonhooks*) and shoe horn (see: *Shoe Horns*). Complete sets are rare and expensive — usually over £150 — but items bought singly are well within the reach of the average collector. A hand mirror, embossed finely with leaves or cherubs' heads costs about £30–£40, and also in this price range are small glass toilet boxes with silver lids, and brushes. When purchasing, it is important to examine the surface for damage. In some cases, only a thin layer of silver was put over the wooden backing, and this is easily torn. Hallmarks should also be checked for dates of manufacture — these are sometimes difficult to locate since they were hidden in the patterns. Ensure, also, that any mirrored surface is in good condition, and not 'flaking' at the edges.

Black ebony sets in plain styles are not expensive. These sometimes have initialled plaques of silver in the form of a shield. The sets usually consisted of a tray (see: *Trinket Sets*) with the appropriate accessories, brushes and hand mirrors. Depending on the number of items in the set, these can be bought for around £15 upwards.

The 1930s saw an increase in the use of plastic, bakelite and celluloid, and hand mirrors, brushes and combs were produced of these materials in great numbers (see: *Plastic* and *Bakelite*). Many

Four-piece silver mounted dressing table set with attractive decoration. £60

were made in pale colours, *eg* pink, green or cream, and had patterns in relief, while others imitated tortoiseshell, amber and ivory.

The 1940s and 50s favoured dressing table sets with embroidered backs in *petit point* style, protected by a clear celluloid or plastic overlay. The articles were edged with decorative gilt coloured metal in elaborate designs. These are still cheap and small sets, usually only three pieces, can be bought at auctions and antique fairs for about £6–£15.

EGG CUPS

Egg cups have been produced throughout the 19th and 20th centuries in a wide range of materials — wood (treen), metal, glass, pottery, porcelain and plastic. So various are their designs and surface motifs that they can be sub-divided into: crested types (see: *Crested China*); those bearing messages from Devon (see: *Motto Ware*); novelties; and commemoratives (see: *Commemorative Ware*) — all of either footed or bucket shape.

Prices range from about £2 to as much as £40, depending on rarity, pattern,

Selection of fine china egg cups, all 19th century. £20–£30 each

material and age. Wooden examples were painted or decorated with poker work. Travelling egg cups had screw-on wooden caps, and some were adorned with transfer-printed scenes in black (see: *Mauchline Ware*). Metal egg cups were produced in silver, silver-plate, aluminium, pressed steel and pewter. Examples were sometimes decoratively embossed or enamelled, but plain plated pieces may be found for as little as £5.

Glass egg cups were usually press-moulded (see: *Press-Moulded Glass*). Some were of chunky form, with a heavy pattern, or were shaped as swans and other birds. These cost about £8–£10 depending on quality. Slag glass egg cups (see: *Press-Moulded Glass*) may be purchased in a similar price range, with their variegated surface effects in grey, mauve and blue.

Plastic egg cups are numerous and come in pale pink, blue and yellow and, being aimed at children, often have hens, chicks, faces and monkeys on them. Bakelite (see: *Bakelite*) ones appeared in dark mottled colours, or were ribbed in bright shades.

Pottery and porcelain egg cups offer most variety to the collector, in terms of their manufacturers and styles. A blue and white example costs from £4 upwards depending on its age, rarity and pattern; novelty cups, perhaps in the form of a teddy bear or hen, can be found for as little as £5.

Egg cup sets or cruets, with matching stands, are much more expensive. A ceramic leaf-shaped stand with flower egg cups by Burgess & Leigh costs about £25, while Victorian complete sets are harder to find, costing from £40–£100 for decorative examples. Ornate silver egg cruets were also produced in the 19th century, adorned with beaded rims and crests, or basket-weave designs.

A matching pair of Crown Staffordshire egg cups, circa 1940, depicting a hunting scene. £10–£12

E

EGG SHELL CHINA

Made in China and Japan, and seldom marked other than 'Japan' or 'foreign', this very thinly potted porcelain is regarded highly by collectors, and is still available at low prices from antique fairs and dealers.

Coffee sets with oriental scenes and flower-shaped finials on the lids sell for about £25–£40 depending on the pattern. Cups, saucers and plates sold as a trio are priced at about £8–£10, while cups and saucers alone can be bought for as little as £3–£5.

The tea cups have wide shallow bowls and if held to the light appear almost translucent. Examples with lithophaned decorations are sought after. When held to the light and examined through the base, the head of a geisha girl can be seen. These cleverly designed examples cost about £8–£10 for a cup and saucer.

ELECTRIC CLOCKS

Early clocks are expensive, and examples made by Ever Ready, Scott, Eureka and the Reason Manufacturing Company cost between £300 and £1000. However, a 'bulle' clock made after 1930

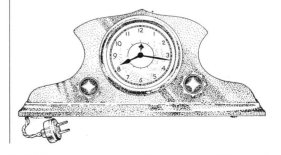

A mains electric clock by Hamilton Sangamo, USA, with mahogany case and silvered dial. £25

by Exide, having a bakelite base (see: *Bakelite*), can be found for purchase between £30 and £50.

Mains electric mantel clocks cost from £10 upwards. Smith's, for example, produced an attractive clock with a veneered case and silver anodized dial, usually marked with the initials 'SEC' (Smith's Electric Company). An American mains clock by Hamilton Sangamo of Illinois, having a handsome, veneered mahogany case and silvered dial, would be priced between £25–£30.

Bakelite-cased clocks of simple design can be found for as little as £6–£8, and are attractive. When purchasing examples, ensure that the shine on the bakelite is intact, and not worn or rubbed. A judicious application of furniture polish can sometimes restore the case, but not always. The collecting of bakelite is on the increase, and prices are expected to rise dramatically for good examples.

EMBOSSERS

These were used by companies for embossing their letterheads. Made in cast iron, they were plain or ornately gilded. The embossing disc can be removed and a modern one made for one's own use. (This will cost about £20 from office stationers.)

The embossing discs are interesting and reveal much about industrialized society. The one illustrated reads: 'Plastic Metallising Ltd,' but more interesting examples can be found. An Edwardian embosser was bought recently for £15, and the disc showed a girl's head with flowing hair and the legend 'Minerva'. Such finds are intriguing. Embossers sell for between £10 and £20, depending on the amount of gilding.

Cast-iron embosser, with gilded pattern of flowers and leaves. £15–£20

EPERGNES

These centrepieces were designed in the 18th and 19th centuries with numerous fittings for displaying fruit, sweetmeats and, later, flowers. Single épergnes of the Victorian period consisted invariably of a trumpet-shaped holder in glass or silver, set into a silver, plated or spelter base. Other varieties were more complex and comprised several trumpets set on a glass or mirrored base. These were used by the Victorians as table decorations, with smaller pieces reserved as vases for flowers.

The single examples with plated or glass stands cost about £15, and were created in clear, coloured or vaseline styles (see: *Vaseline Glass*). A spelter example may be priced from £20–£30, and a pair in fine condition about £50–£60.

Larger, multi-trumpet épergnes were frequently of vaseline or cranberry glass (see: *Cranberry Glass*), or combinations of the two, and cost between £150 and £300 depending on the complexity of the arrangement. Some had hanging baskets, in addition to the trumpets, suspended from curved metal supports. The trumpets appeared variously — either plain, or with frilled edges and/or trails of glass wound spirally around the stems in a contrasting shade. Cranberry glass was decorated frequently with clear glass trimmings, while vaseline was edged with green, cranberry or turquoise, sometimes juxtaposed with 'sugar cane' twisted rods which radiated upwards from the base. These extravagant styles reflect admirably 'high Victorian' tastes of *c.*1860–80.

Because the price of large épergnes is so prohibitive, some collectors have concentrated on the single trumpet-like

Vaseline glass epergne decorated with green frilling, standing about 2 feet high. £250–£300

vases, priced from about £15 each depending on their size, colour and decoration.

These smaller pieces are more easily displayed than their giant counterparts of up to 30 inches tall.

ETUIS

These needlework cases or small boxes were made to protect needles and other accessories for sewing, which were expensive and precious. By the 18th century, needles had become cheaper and plentiful, and cases more decorative.

Wooden ones were usually of cylindrical shape, although square, oblong and ovoid forms were also created. Examples were decorated with hand-painted motifs, poker work, or with transfer-printed scenes (see: *Mauchline Ware*) and these may be found for purchase from £15 upwards. Tunbridgeware cases (see: *Tunbridge-ware*) are more expensive and cost around £40.

Etuis were also made of precious

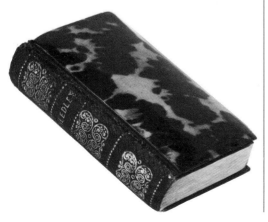

Tortoiseshell needlecase in the shape of a book. £30–£35

metals and stones from *c.*1750 onwards, sometimes inlaid with pieces of ivory and mother-of-pearl (see: *Small Silver*). The latter material was often engraved with delicate floral sprays and other motifs, and pretty examples cost from about £60 upwards. Silver cases were oblong, square or cylindrical, embossed or chased with rich surface patterns, and these cost from £50 upwards, depending on their age and appeal. Unusual shapes are also to be found such as figures, book-shaped boxes and other novelties. Beadwork examples are rare and usually collectable, and are usually priced from £25 upwards (see: *Beadwork*).

During the 19th century, one of the most popular materials for needle cases was brass, and the firm of W. Avery produced a great many. These were intended to hold packets of needles, and appeared of oblong or square form, although unusual shapes such as scallop shells and butterflies can also be found. These usually cost from £40.

Needlecase packets or folders were made of card, paper or leather, usually in the shape of a book or wallet. Some were decorated with beads, scraps of material, or had hand-painted flower pictures. Prices for these vary between £15 and £20, although simple paper packets can be found for under £3.

EYE BATHS

A selection of eye baths in different shapes and colours ranging between £5 and £10

G lass eye baths were made in three different shapes — stemmed, unstemmed and of reservoir form. The latter, with its fishbowl base, appeared in about 1880 with the introduction of new production methods for pressed glass (see: *Press Moulded Glass*). Previously, glass eye baths had been hand blown in clear glass but with the craze for coloured glass in the second half of the 19th century, eye baths were made in dark royal blue, green (the two colours most found today), amber, dark and light turquoise, as well as in clear glass. The reservoir eye bath was made in clear glass, blue, green and amber. Prices vary from £5 for a clear glass example to £8–£10 for dark royal blue, and as much as £20 for the rarer turquoise colours.

The unstemmed baths are cheaper than the stemmed or reservoir types, but these should not be confused with the royal blue glass liners used in silver or plated cruet containers. If in doubt, fit the eye bath to the eye. If it fits the eye socket comfortably and makes a good seal, it is the genuine article.

FAIRINGS

These small porcelain figural groups date from about 1860 and were made until the end of the century. They derive their name from the fact that they were given away as prizes and souvenirs at fairgrounds. Most are about 4 inches high and were made at Pössneck in Germany for the British market. Early examples are unmarked, and sometimes hollow, but later fairings bear the words 'Made in Germany'.

A typical Victorian fairing bearing the risqué question 'Shall We Sleep First, My Love?'. £40

Although of porcelain, fairings were indifferently made and the modelling was rather crude. They were intended to be amusing and sometimes *risqué*, and most bear a succinct and humorous message. Occasionally, identical figure groups are found with different wordings. Reproductions are now being made, so it is important to check for signs of wear or surface crazing. If the fairing is sold cheaply, ensure that it is not a reproduction before buying, thinking it is

F

a bargain. Many examples have been restored, so again, careful examination is advisable. Small repairs, however, do not necessarily decrease the value.

One of the best-known and most frequently seen fairings is the one entitled 'Last Into Bed Puts Out The Light' (sometimes known as 'The Last In Bed To Put Out The Light'). This shows a night-capped couple about to climb into bed, with a candle on the counterpane. This model sells for about £40. 'Naughty Words' shows a couple remonstrating with a parrot and costs £40–£60. 'United We Stand, Divided We Fall' shows a pair of top-hatted drunks, and is priced between £50 and £60.

Fairings which feature people on bicycles usually sell for between £100 and £300 (even if restored). Pieces in the form of match holders are cheaper than figure groups (see: *Match Holders and Strikers*) and cost from £30 upwards. Untitled fairings start at about £20–£25, although many others bearing slogans — and depicting a variety of subjects including 'Little Boy Blue', 'Little Red Riding Hood', children and couples — can be found for purchase from £40–£65. The appeal and rarity of the fairing are the guidelines to price, with sporting and travelling subjects commanding the highest sums.

FAIRY TALES

The first English edition of *Grimm's Fairy Tales* was published in 1823, followed by Hans Christian Andersen's fairy stories in 1846, and new editions of *The Sleeping Beauty* and *Cinderella*. Indeed, the late 19th and early 20th centuries were a golden era in children's book illustrations. Famous artists such as Dulac, Arthur Rackham, Burne-Jones,

Richard Dadd, Heath Robinson and Richard Doyle created some of their finest works for books on fairies. These first editions are now very collectable and range in price from about £40 to £150.

In 1892 Andrew Lang published the first of his 'coloured' fairy books. There were twelve in all, each individually titled such as *The Green Fairy Book*, *The Yellow Fairy Book*, and so on, with illustrations by H. J. Ford. These ran into several editions and it is still possible to pick up later copies (for example, the 1927 publication) for about £20 each and build up the set.

A great many book illustrators had their work issued as prints, and those by Dulac and Rackham, for example, are often on sale at antique fairs. The illustrator Margaret Tarrant is extremely popular with collectors of fairy prints, and much of her work can still be found at very reasonable prices — from about £10 upwards, depending on the subject.

Illustration from The Green Fairy Book *edited by Andrew Lang, drawings by H. J. Ford. 1927 edition £20*

FANS

It wasn't until the 18th century that the fan came into its own as a fashion accessory that was both functional and beautiful. The Chinese were the exponents of the rigid fan from *c*.1400, and Queen Elizabeth I is portrayed holding a rigid fan of feathers. The Europeans, however, developed the folding fan to a high standard of excellence, with France the leader of fashionable tastes. Here, the richest fabrics and materials were used: mother-of-pearl, ivory, and gem-studded sticks supported the highly decorated leaves or mounts. The guard was invariably ornate, perhaps of chased gold encrusted with jewels. These fans were the prerogative of the wealthy, and indispensable dress accessories for balls and other formal occasions.

Among the most popular was the brisé fan. This was designed without a mount, the sticks and guard being held together by silk or ribbon slotted through holes at the top and fastened by a rivet.

In the mid-19th century the 'Mandarin' fan gained popularity. This

Left: A sequin decorated muslin fan. £20–£25. Right: A black silk fan with ebony sticks, decorated with gold sequins. £22–£28

was made for the Chinese export market and the paper mount was painted with an oriental scene. The guards were of tortoiseshell, ivory, sandalwood or painted lacquered wood. Other oriental styles were adopted during the 1880s–90s with the craze for *japonaiserie*, adorned with Eastern-style scenes, flowers and bird motifs.

As fans became more widely used, lithographed examples came into being. These were cheaper to produce and a variety of designs could be printed on the mounts quickly and easily. This idea was adopted wholeheartedly by advertisers in the late 19th century who gave fans away to their customers adorned with their printed sales' messages. These were usually of folding form, but sometimes the 'cockade' fan was used. This was opened by bringing the guard sticks together from the bottom to the top to form a circle.

Materials used for the mounts varied enormously: silk, satin, gauze and net, with painted, embroidered or spangled designs were all popular. In the mid-1800s lace became fashionable, and fans were designed frequently with lace panels to complement bridal gowns. Feathers reappeared at this time, and when the Victorian debutante was presented at court, complete with a plume of ostrich feathers in her hair, she would often carry a matching fan. Neater and less opulent examples were adorned with humming bird feathers, or the angled tips of peacock feathers.

Horn fans were made during Regency times and these were either of brisé or cockade form. The horn was plunged into boiling water to make it malleable and more translucent, after which the surface was painted and decorated, and the guards pierced or gilded.

Prices for fans vary according to age,

rarity, and quality. Early fans are obviously expensive and can cost hundreds of pounds. But for the beginner collector, examples are still available at reasonable cost. An ostrich feather fan can be bought for as little as £15; lace fans from around £20; and horn examples — possibly because they are less prone to damage, and therefore exist in relatively large numbers — are available from around £30 upwards.

More expensive examples are also found displaying delicate surface decorations.

FLAT IRONS & OTHERS

Two flat irons of different sizes, made in cast iron. £4–£5

The flat iron became widespread in the late 19th century and retained its popularity until the mid-1930s. Made with a hollow handle and a tempered steel face, the irons (used in pairs) were placed in front of the fire until they had reached the desired temperature. Known also as 'sad irons' — the name a corruption of 'solid' — they were made in different sizes and marked according to weight. There was no standardization of weights, however, and as a result apparently similar irons from a range of makers would bear different numbers. These run from 1 to 12, although sometimes 14 is found, and the number is stamped on the iron along with the maker's name. Some collectors aim for a whole series by the same manufacturer. Flat irons will cost from about £4 to £5. Rusty examples can be cleaned with grate polish, but avoid any that are pitted or where the metal appears to be eaten away.

Box irons were in existence before flat irons and date from the 18th century onwards. Both types, however, were in production during later periods. Box models were made of iron with a hollow interior. A heated slug of metal would be slipped into the hollow by means of a sliding or hinged flap on either heel or top. Charcoal irons were also made on the box principle with fuel being burned inside the hollow body. English and Continental examples had holes at the sides to allow the fumes to escape, and later models were fitted with a short funnel near the handle. Prices for these start at about £10, while early box irons of *c*.1800 can be purchased in the region of £20–£25.

FOUNTAIN PENS & PROPELLING PENCILS

The famous names in pens are Parker and Waterman, both of whom invented a type of self-filling pen. J. J. Parker was the first to manufacture fountain pens in 1823 but these were prone to leakage and it took another 60 years before Waterman brought out an improved model based on the capillary attraction system in 1883.

Fountain pen shapes varied little over the years, although a few new materials were introduced, such as: bakelite — the mottled variety being popular; vulcanite, and other plastics (see: *Bakelite* and *Plastic*); and base metals in imitation of silver and gold. Small pens were made for women to carry in their handbags and these were attractively decorated with silver or gold bands, and mother-of-pearl veneers.

Most turn-of-the-century pens are expensive, but examples from the 1930s start at around £4 for a Conway Stewart

Propelling pencil with ivorine barrel. £10

in pink and black mottled bakelite.

Propelling pencils were invented earlier than fountain pens. Samuel Mordan brought out his Everpointed pencil in 1822 and the factory stayed in production until 1941. There is more variety in pencils than pens, with a greater range in size. They were made in silver and gold and other metals, and later in plastic. Some had mother-of-pearl barrels with end-pieces in gold. Others were made flat with a ring on one end for hanging from a chatelaine (a belt worn around the waist with chains or cords on which were suspended such things as scissors, etuis (see: *Etuis*), keys, *etc*).

Tiny propelling pencils were made for the handbag and these can be bought quite reasonably. A silver pencil costs about £10 upwards, while an example in gold by Sampson Mordan may be priced in the region of £60. Silver slide-action pens and pencils, for example those by Joseph Willmore or Gabriel Riddle of early 19th-century date, are more costly at about £100 each.

GAMES

1930s fountain pen in bakelite black case. £4

The late 19th and early 20th centuries were golden eras for indoor games, when many new versions of dice board games were introduced from the Orient. Ludo, based on the Indian game *pachisi*, was patented in 1896 and became an immediate success. Mah Jong was brought from China in the 1880s or 90s, and Halma was played on a chequerboard with pegs of wood or ivory. Solitaire, another Victorian favourite, had coloured marbles set on a polished wooden base — a game which now commands a high price, costing from £30–£70 depending on its size and decorative appeal. Complete

Games complete with their boxes command higher prices than those without. These two games will cost £10–£15

sets with matching marbles have become increasingly difficult to find, and the glass balls should be examined for chips or damage.

Draughts and chess have been played for centuries and early chess sets with elaborately carved figures in wood and ivory may cost thousands of pounds. Small sets, however, in simple wooden boxes can be found for about £20. Dominoes in ebony with ivory spots are also reasonably priced, although it is important to check that the set is complete — there should be 28 pieces. Cribbage boards, often made like boxes to hold a pack of cards, and hinged in the middle to open out flat, can be found in attractive woods. Examples cost about £20 if in good condition, and well patterned. Tunbridgeware boxes (see: *Tunbridgeware*) are more expensive, priced from about £40 upwards depending on the intricacy of the pattern.

Card games were popular with children, and many were intended to be of educational value. The cards often followed themes, with titles such as 'Celebrated Poets', although amusing sets such as 'Comic Families' were produced

— the forerunner of the modern 'Happy Families' game (see: *Playing Cards*). Mah Jong continued to be fashionable in England in the 1920s, and backgammon was revived in the 30s, having come to Europe in the 12th century.

The Victorians, always keen on educating their children, produced a plethora of jigsaw puzzles. Early puzzles were of simple shapes (since sophisticated cutting techniques had not yet been developed), and covered a wide range of historical and literary subjcts such as: the Kings and Queens of England, the Progress of Ship Building; biblical and historical tables; and a series of maps featuring the countries and continents of the world. By the 1930s wooden puzzles had given way to cardboard since the latter material could be cut easily and more intricately. Mid- and late-Victorian puzzles cost from £15–£20 depending on their condition and whether they are boxed. Jumble sales and flea markets are a good source for these, but check that all the pieces are there.

GREETINGS CARDS

A selection of Christmas cards priced between £3 and £7

The first Christmas card was made for Henry Cole in 1843, designed by John Horsley. Up to a thousand cards were made, but it was not until 1862 that the first commercial Christmas card was produced. Santa Claus, robins, holly, mistletoe, bells, plum puddings, angels and cherubs all featured.

Christmas cards appeared in two forms: of folding variety, or as postcards. The latter are more easily found for purchase today and can be bought from 50 pence upwards, although examples which reveal a different scene when held up to the light cost about £10 each.

The folding card became elaborate by the 1890s with the addition of silk or satin padding, fringing and lace. Double cards opened to display nativity scenes. Cut out cards were shaped like plum puddings, stars, flowers, fans, leaves or vases, and were sprinkled with glitter. These cost from £3 upwards.

Valentine cards appealed to the sentimental Victorians, and they were made from the 1830s onwards with silk or satin hearts, lace flounces and frills. Some had special Valentine envelopes which were produced after 1840, with the introduction of uniform postal charges. Numerous romantic messages were expressed such as 'My heart will be ever thine', or 'Maiden, thy little heart to let'. The more ornate the card, the more expensive, with prices starting from about £8– £10 upwards. Simpler varieties may be found for about £3. An elaborate card in the shape of a banknote, drawn on the Lover's Banking Company, costs about £12–£15. Later cards from the 1930s are much cheaper, starting at about £1 each.

Birthday cards of the Victorian era are simple in design and cost as little as £2 or £3, while examples of later periods can be found for 50 pence. Collectors of birthday cards often concentrate on particular themes such as 21st celebrations, and subjects of humorous, romantic or family content. A card with the words 'You are four today', depicting a rabbit and teddy bear and dating from the 1930s, costs about 50 pence.

Many famous illustrators created cards during the 19th and 20th centuries. Kate Greenaway's works are highly collectable, as are those by Margaret Tarrant (see: *Fairy Tales and Illustrations*), Mabel Lucy Attwell, Louis Wain and his cats (see: *Wain, Louis*), Walter Crane, and Horatio Coudray. Cards featuring Mickey Mouse are also popular with collectors today.

A collectable Easter card costing about £8–£10

HAIR COMBS

Hair styles became very elaborate in the 1860s with the hair being held in a beaded net and caught in a low chignon. Hair combs were essential to hold this in place and one can find hinged examples from this period. The decorative cresting of the comb could then be adjusted to the style of the wearer.

Many 19th-century combs were electro-gilded and decorated with pearls, coral, gold, silver or tortoiseshell — with tiny pieces either beaded and sewn on to the surface, or hung in festoons of drops.

By 1890 when Art Nouveau was at its height, stylized combs were ornamented with gemstones such as amethyst, moonstone, turquoise, opal or lapis lazuli. Horn and tortoiseshell were used extensively during this period, rendered into flowing shapes and embellished with butterflies, flowers and stylized female forms. Some pieces were enamelled in various shades of brown, blue and orange, or appeared with applied beaten silver decorations in the Arts and Crafts style. These are the most costly combs to collect and will be from about £60 upwards.

Synthetic materials were widely used from the mid-19th century (see: *Plastic* and *Bakelite*). Casein was used to imitate ivory, vulcanite for jet, and tortoiseshell and amber were also copied. The 'ivory' combs were moulded into filigree or lace-like patterns, with vulcanite reserved frequently for flower shapes. These synthetic combs are attractive and inexpensive with prices beginning at around £8. Silver combs with ornate headings, however, will cost from £30 upwards; and those of bold Art Nouveau design in horn and other materials may be in excess of £80.

A varied selection of hair combs and ornaments, made in bakelite, tortoiseshell, mother-of-pearl and horn. Prices range between about £8 for the small black bakelite comb (top right) to over £100 for the pair of combs at the bottom of the picture, made of horn and decorated with silver and abalone

The 1920s gave rise to exotic fashions and Spanish-style shawls and high combs with large decorative crests were favoured. These will sell for about £12 today. With the advent of shorter hair styles combs declined in popularity and later examples tend to be small and discreetly fashioned.

HAT PINS & HOLDERS

These were introduced in great numbers in the late 1800s when the fashion for large hats began. The hatpins could be as much as 12 inches in length, ornamented with materials such as silver, ivory, jet, mother-of-pearl, gold encrusted with gems and semi-precious stones, and ceramics. Silver pins appeared with great variety, such as those produced by Charles Horner hallmarked Chester between 1906 and 1913, or marked 'C. H. Sterling'. Horner's thistle pins adorned with glass flowers cost £30 or more and are highly collectable. Other fine hatpin manufacturers were Shrimpton and Co, and Pearce and Thompson.

Fanciful hatpins were ornamented with butterfly heads, leaves, owls, parrots, flowers and abstract swirling shapes in the Art Nouveau style. The designs were highlighted with beads of turquoise, pearl, jet, amber or coloured glass. These range in price from £3 to £5 for paste examples, to over £50 for pins in

A selection of hallmarked silver pins ranging between £12 and £30

gemstones and precious metals. During the 1920s and 30s synthetic materials were also used (see: *Plastic* and *Bakelite*), and sequins, shells, and imitations of mother-of-pearl, amber and tortoiseshell were employed in a lively manner — ranging in price from £2 to £20.

The pins were stored in special holders — as various in materials and styles as the hatpins themselves, and made of precious metals, glass, copper, raffia, straw and reed. Examples were produced in England from *c.*1860–1924 — some resemble giant pepper pots, sugar castors, or candlesticks that have lost their upper rims. Porcelain and pottery examples are collectable in their own right and cost from £12 to £15.

HORN OBJECTS

This attractive material has the benefit of becoming plastic when heated, and so can be pressed or moulded into a variety of shapes. Horn beakers have been used for centuries and are still being made, while a variety of small objects was produced from the 1800s including: buttonhooks (see: *Buttonhooks*); matchboxes and cases (see: *Vesta cases*); snuff boxes; spoons; shoe horns (see: *Shoe Horns*); handles for cutlery and carving sets; cut throat razors; ladles; fans; and jewellery. The smooth, even surface of horn appears in variegated shades of creamy beige, yellow, greenish-tan and brown, and some of the finest pieces display these subtle, merging hues streaked across their surfaces.

Prices vary according to the type of article, and its decorative appeal. A fine cased carving set of Sheffield steel with staghorn handles and silver mounts costs from £50–£70. Cut throat razors in

Four horn beakers from the 19th century. About £10 each for the plain examples, £15–£20 for the engraved one

buffalo horn, shoe horns in oxhorn, and staghorn handled buttonhooks can all be found for between £10 and £20. Much more expensive are the silver-banded horn beakers of 18th and 19th century manufacture, although unadorned specimens of later date can cost as little as £10. Pieces should be examined for wear and distortion — and those with warped sides and/or cracks are best avoided. Engraved beakers are more valuable than plain ones, and for this reason many antique specimens are found with newly-engraved surfaces. Again, look for signs of wear on the engraved designs.

For further reading on the subject, Paula Hardwick's book *Discovering Horn* is recommended.

HORSE BRASSES

They began life centuries ago as amulets or charms against the evil eye. In the early 1800s casting techniques meant that large quantities of elaborately-designed horse brasses could be made easily and relatively cheaply. The sun and crescent moon figured largely in the designs, as did the cross, fashioned in either the Maltese or Greek form.

Farmers chose wheatsheaf patterns, sporting types would favour a running fox or a gamebird. Brasses were made bearing trade designs, such as a beer barrel or flour sack, while regions of the country were represented with devices such as the Staffordshire Knot, the Cotswold Woolbales, or the Wiltshire Dolphin.

Complete sets of horse brasses mounted on their original harnesses will cost over £60, but individual brasses will cost from £25 each.

Some attractive horse brasses priced from about £25 each

HUMMEL FIGURES

Two Hummel figures, both from the 1950s, from £22 each

Manufactured by W. Goebel of West Germany, these figurines were adapted from sketches created by Sister Maria Innocentia (formerly Berta Hummel) of Bavaria. The German factory began producing Hummel figures in 1935, and the first backstamp shows an incised or stamped crown with the initials 'W.G.' below. Later marks, from 1946 onwards, show various bumble bee motifs (Goebel means bee in German) flying between the upper strokes of a 'V'. Some of the figures are still being made, so it is important to check the backstamps carefully for dates.

Over 200 different figures, in various sizes, were produced, as well as plates, bells, ashtrays, book ends, candle holders, lidded boxes, musical boxes, nativity sets, plaques, table lamps, and wall vases.

The figures are instantly recognizable with their soft colours and semi-matt glazes. Groups of children are seen occupied in domestic pursuits such as sweeping the floor, feeding the ducks, or playing the accordion. Other types depict postmen, bakers and musicians going about their business.

Prices for these start from £25 for a 1950s example, to £45 and up for a 1930s/1940s figure. The collector should view as many specimens as possible, since there appear to be great variations in price. For example, a Hummel wall vase was seen recently at an antique fair for £110, while a similar piece was found for £65. Pieces with minor damage can be found for about £12.

Although Hummel figures were made exclusively by W. Goebel, the factory produced other items as well — hence, not all articles marked 'Goebel' are part of the Hummel range.

INKSTANDS

Originally called a standish, silver inkstands have survived from *c.*1630, and were intended for use on the writing table or desk. Early examples of casket form or equipped with a tray and accessories cost £400–£500, but later pieces in porcelain, silver-plate and other materials are more affordable. Nineteenth-century inkstands consist invariably of a tray, sometimes with a carrying handle, one or two inkwells (for red, blue or black ink), a pen tray or rack, and a small lidded box or drawer for stamps.

Some attractive examples in brass may appear of simple design, with just one inkwell and an indentation for the pen. These will cost about £18–£25 although decorative pieces with embossing, or pierced with Arts and Crafts motifs, may cost more. Small stands were also produced in polished wood or ebony, with a brass handle and shallow drawer for stamps, nibs or spare pens. These cost about £40.

Pressed glass examples can be found in clear glass and these are relatively inexpensive at £12–£15. During the Art Deco period, bakelite stands and coloured glass inkwells in geometric styles were produced, sometimes placed on mirror glass bases. These are usually priced from £15 upwards (see: *Press Moulded Glass* and *Bakelite*).

A more unusual type of inkstand is the 'elephant' stand. This was made of ebonized wood with decorative white spots forming the pattern. There are always at least two elephants on the stand, sometimes as many as six or eight. The ink pots comprise small wooden containers, and there is usually a lidded stamp box. Sometimes there is a pen rack

☆ **BARGAIN BUY**
Bakelite inkstand with two inkwells. In good condition it will cost about £10–£12. This one was bought at a flea market for only £4. Look out for bakelite examples as this is a good field for the beginner

at the rear of the stand which resembles a ladder with its slotted metal bars, although occasionally this has been replaced by a watch stand (see: *Watch Stands*). Elephant stands sell for between £30 and £40 in good condition. When purchasing, ensure that the elephant tusks are intact, and that the stamp box lid is not missing. If glass inkwells are to be used on the stand, check the brass corners and underside of the lids for damage.

Porcelain inkwells and stands offer the collector great variety, and numerous decorative examples were produced by all the major factories from *c.*1800 onwards. Apart from the traditional tray shape, fitted with two apertures either side to contain the inkwells, other novel forms were introduced. Wedgwood created barrel-shaped inkstands in jasperware, while Worcester designed pieces of drum-form during the 'Barr, Flight and Barr' period of the early 19th century. Coalport specialized in floral decorated wares from *c.*1800–40, and inkwells were made with large blossoms in relief at the base. Minton devised many attractive marbelized styles for desk accessories, and such sets often include tapersticks (for writing at night) and pouncepots. The prices of porcelain inkstands vary enormously depending on the manufacturer and rarity of the piece.

INKWELLS

These come in a wide range of designs, from pottery and porcelain greyhounds, faces, and animals of all descriptions, to simple round and square inkwells in heavy glass.

Glass inkwells have either matching tops in cut glass, or silver, brass or other

Victorian porcelain inkwell. £15–£20

metal lids. Souvenir inkwells usually consist of two ink containers fixed on a boat-shaped stand, featuring a sepia scenic photograph enclosed in a glass medallion between the two.

Glass inkwells range from about £6 for a plain model, to about £30 for a finely cut example with matching stopper. Those which incorporate silver, or unusual pieces which display a watch under the lid, may cost up to £100.

Pewter inkwells of the early 20th century in a 'capstan' design, with a saucer for catching drips cost from £20 — and more if of earlier date. Brass inkwells will cost £15 upwards. Check both pewter and brass for splits, cracks and dents.

Travelling inkwells were popular during the late 18th and 19th centuries, before the widespread use of fountain pens. The cases for these were round or square fitted in leather or brass with glass bottles inside. Often these were ingeniously made with spring-released lids to ensure a watertight fit during travel.

A Scottish advertisement of 1775 recommended these portable sets highly as the 'best Edinburgh inkpots, for the pocket', priced then at a few shillings. These still appear in plentiful supply today, and range in price from about £15 to £70 for a Regency period leather covered case.

Leather covered brass travelling inkwell. £18

JAM POTS

Two jam pots from the 1930s. The one with a butterfly finial is in shades of pink and mauve (£15), the Royal Winton example to the front of the picture is from their 'Elf' series. £20–£25

These are popular with collectors, and some very pretty china and pottery jam pots can be found for purchase dating from the 1920s and 1930s. Round ones for marmalade resemble oranges, and honey pots were made by Clarice Cliff and others in the shape of a beehive with a bumble bee as the finial on the lid. Royal Winton (Grimwades) made fanciful jam pots with elves or lakeland scenes on them, or shaped like Tudor cottages, while Royal Venton created examples in deep pink with butterfly finials. These cost about £20 each. Carlton produced jam and honey pots in characteristic style, decorated with the leaves and flowers of the foxglove and primrose (see: *Carlton Ware*). These are about £14. Crown Staffordshire, Aynsley and other makers of fine china (see: *Coffee Cans* and *Cups and Saucers*) all produced jam pots in lively designs. Many are straight sided with floral patterns. The Devon potteries (see: *Torquay and Devon Pottery*) made jam pots in blue with kingfishers on the side, and in mottoware with its cream background and brown writing (see: *Motto Ware*). The majority of the above range in price from £10–£15. They make attractive displays, or can be used for their original purpose at breakfast or tea.

Marmalade pot shaped like an orange. The registered mark underneath gives it a date of 1878. £12–£15

JARDINIERES

The plant holder or jardinière reached its height of popularity in Victorian times, when plants were taken out of conservatories and displayed in windows and interiors. Examples have been collected eagerly ever since.

The best-known maker was Royal Doulton and they produced splendid pottery jardinières with matching pedestal stands. These sets cost between £300 and £400, but the jardinière alone can sometimes be found for about £100, or more for a particularly splendid, well-patterned specimen.

Bretby was another well-known manufacturer, and a jardinière from this factory costs about £80. Signed pieces by Henry Tooth or William Ault can be more expensive.

Unmarked pottery jardinières vary in price according to their style and decoration. Edwardian examples with Art Nouveau designs are most sought after, usually priced over £100. A turn-of-the-century jardinière in a soft maroon shade, with a hairline crack, was bought for £3 at a boot sale (see illustration), although if intended for use pieces should be in good condition and watertight.

Any damage, however slight, will reduce the price, and it is worth remembering that any small chips around the rim can be hidden by foliage.

Miniature jardinières or plant holders of about 6 inches high can also be found, displaying rich Imari patterns. Many were produced by the Staffordshire factories in the second half of the 19th century to hold small plants. Examples can be displayed most attractively on mantelpieces as decorative ornaments, and can be purchased in the region of £15–£25.

☆ **BARGAIN BUY**
A superb Minton jardiniere. Would normally cost about £80–£90, but a small amount of damage reduced the price to £40

☆ **BARGAIN BUY**
This attractive jardiniere in maroon was bought for only £3 at a boot sale. It has a hairline crack which is barely noticeable

JELLY MOULDS -COPPER

Copper moulds can fetch high prices, especially those found in gleaming condition and with interesting shapes. Some examples with pronounced swirl patterns and other rich relief designs can cost in excess of £100. The moulds were tinned inside (since copper is a poisonous substance) and often appear dull and grey. Some copper moulds were taller than their pottery counterparts (see next entry), and were rendered into fanciful forms such as the favourite fish shapes. These are finely detailed, with the scales standing out in relief. Turreted or castellated shapes are also highly prized, and make splendid displays in country-style kitchens and dining rooms.

Prices for copper moulds of plain design start at about £40, although early and decorative examples can fetch much more. Condition is an important factor in determining value, and if the exterior is split, torn or dented this is usually reflected by a comparatively lower price. Small dents, however, which detract little from the overall form and decoration of the piece, are generally considered insignificant.

A small copper mould circa 1870, just over 3 inches high. £40

JELLY MOULDS - POTTERY

Jellies were made in great numbers in Victorian times and an early copy of *Mrs Beeton's Household Management* lists no less than 178 recipes for sweet and savoury jellies. A wide variety of decorative moulds was produced, made of copper (see previous entry) or of white or cream-coloured earthenware. The shapes and patterns for pottery moulds reflect an enormous diversity. Oval moulds are seen mostly in a blancmange shape, but examples were also made of square, round, turreted, and block form. The patterns showed fruit, leaves, beehives, and various animals for savoury jellies to accompany lamb, fish or turkey. Some moulds were multi-tiered, so that different coloured jellies could be poured in to form contrasting layers.

Makers who stamped or marked their moulds included Wedgwood, Minton, Maling, Grimwades, Davenport and Copeland, and it is sometimes possible to date specimens from these marks. Such examples cost from £25–£40. Unmarked moulds are cheaper, as are plainer pieces which can be found from about £5. Severe surface staining detracts from the value.

A handsome creamware mould from the late 18th century, showing a pattern of fruit in the base. £40–£50

JET JEWELLERY

The heyday for this jewellery was after the death of Prince Albert in 1861 when Queen Victoria plunged the court — and the country — into strict mourning.

Jet is an organic material, of opaque black appearance, derived from the fossilized remains of trees. Large quantities of jet were mined near Whitby in Yorkshire, although the mineral was found elsewhere in England — and even imported from Spain during the height of its popularity.

Each piece was hand carved and this led to a great variety of patterns. Brooches appeared in simple 'bar' styles decorated with flowers or names (see: *Name Brooches*), or were formed into bold medallions and cameos as much as 6 inches across. These large brooches were used for pinning shawls, rather than for use on dresses, and sometimes were adorned additionally with carved mother-of-pearl plaques and ivory appliqués. Some of the grander examples had earrings and necklaces *en suite*. The earrings were designed invariably for pierced ears, composed of boldly carved drops in geometric or floral styles, up to 3 inches in length. Necklaces were produced in the form of beads or chains. The beads were faceted, or carved with flowers and leaves, the two most popular patterns being the rose and fern. Chains had round, square, plain or faceted links, often with a large hook at the bottom for attaching a pendant or double-sided locket of polished jet.

Alternatively, some pendants were worn suspended on a piece of velvet ribbon. The majority were of rounded shape and followed the decorative styles of brooches, but lockets fitted with oval glass interiors for containing photographs, or faced with glass on the reverse to contain the hair of a loved one, were also fashionable.

French jet is another name for black glass and is distinguished from 'Whitby jet' by its cold, brittle and glassy appearance. French jet was used extensively for jewellery during the late Victorian and Edwardian periods, and many fine pieces were made displaying heavily-faceted and sparkling surfaces. Bog oak was another material employed contemporaneously in keeping with the fashion for black jewellery. This fossilized wood, however, is woody in appearance, being dark brown rather than black, and lacking the high polish of jet. Many fanciful pieces were made in this material including: earrings with acorn drops; ornately carved bracelets and necklaces depicting castles and scenes; and brooches in the form of hands, floral wreaths, doves and tennis rackets.

The prices for 'Whitby jet' jewellery have increased greatly in recent years, and examples are popular with collectors and fashion enthusiasts. Large and well-carved brooches and pendants are usually priced from £40–£100, while small 'bar-type' pins can be found from only £15–£25.

Serpent bracelets, featuring faceted pieces and a snake's head, of gently-coiled form, are highly sought after and have an exotic appeal. These often cost in excess of £90, although bracelets strung on to elastic cords with simple flower motifs may be less. Earrings are very popular with collectors, particularly boldly carved pieces displaying cameo portraits, mosaics or complex geometric designs. Long and dramatic pairs with gold or silver wires (and retaining their original tops) are usually priced from £65–£150.

When purchasing, the collector should examine the surface carefully for damage

A jet bracelet, the sections faceted and carved and strung on elastic to resemble a snake. Each piece is angled to fit into the next, thus giving the desired curvature, and fitting closely on the wearer's arm. £40

since jet is brittle and prone to chipping and cracking. A number of pieces have been restored, by grinding down a chipped part, or by filling and painting the surface in black. These renewed areas are usually discernible on close inspection.

French jet jewellery tends to be less expensive, and sharply faceted earrings and brooches in the form of flowers and stars range from about £10–£30. Elaborate necklaces, however, with decorative drops may cost up to £100. Bog oak remains modestly priced, and a wide selection can be found for under £15.

JEWELLERY BOXES

☆ **BARGAIN BUY**
Attractive jewellery boxes can be found for as little as £8 or £9, and are good value for money. This one is covered in black leather-look paper and the two removable trays and the interior are lined with green silk

These are attractive and functional, and may be found from the Regency period onwards in a variety of woods such as walnut, mahogany, rosewood and coramandel. Boxes of the latter two materials tend to be the most expensive, ranging in price from about £80–£100. Examples are either plain, or inlaid with mother-of-pearl or brass stringing. Sometimes there is a small brass or silver shield set in to the lid for the purposes of initialling, and metal mounted corners were added for protection. Leather boxes were made more decorative by the addition of heavily embossed silver appliqués placed on the lids and sides, surmounted by a small carrying handle. These cost about £60–£70.

More modestly priced are the mock leather jewel boxes in black, dark green, dark blue, or maroon. These are padded and lined with silk and velvet, and fitted with one or two removable trays with a slotted section for rings and bar brooches, a circular partition for a fob watch, and a compartment for bracelets, necklaces, etc.

These boxes are greatly under-valued and make useful adjuncts to the dressing table, priced at about £15.

Some boxes have a 'Bramah' lock, and examples stamped with this name can fetch about £50 or more. The presence of the original keys also increases the value. It is important to ensure that these are in fine working order, enabling the box to be locked and unlocked.

JUGS

These come in all sizes, from tiny cream jugs for use with 'bachelor's breakfast sets' to the ewers that come with washstand sets. But at present, it is the brightly coloured jugs of the 1930s that are highly collectable. These were made in various sizes but the most popular with collectors today are those between 5 and 10 inches high, manufactured by firms such as Burgess & Leigh. Their jugs, invariably coloured bright yellow, appeared with variously modelled handles shaped like dragons,

Two early Victorian Staffordshire jugs with transfer printed designs. The one on the left is brightly coloured with a good design (£30), the other is less attractive and will be cheaper at about £12

K

*Small helmet-shaped
jug in blue and white
(9 inches high).
£25–£30*

squirrels, kingfishers, parrots, even tennis
players and golfers. They are always
clearly marked underneath, and cost
£20–£25.

Clarice Cliff designed novelty jugs
adorned with exotic motifs such as the
flamingo, with its neck curving round to
form the handle (see: *Cliff, Clarice*).
Falcon Ware produced a jug in the form
of a bird bath on a stand, with a pigeon
resting on the top of the handle. This
model sells for about £25–£30.

Other lively pieces were created by:
Grimwades, who produced a garden
series, the jugs almost conical in shape
with twisted tree-like handles; Wade
Heath who produced flower decorated
jugs, and ones bearing Walt Disney
designs; and S. Fielding (see *Crown Devon
Ware*) who made delightful musical jugs
for Etonians. These jugs start from £30.

Beswick jugs in soft pastel colours are
very under-rated and fine examples can
be found below £15. Charlotte Rhead's
tube-lined wares are highly sought after
(see: *Rhead, Charlotte*) and her small jugs
of about 4 inches high will cost around
£30.

*Kettles — See Barge Kettles, page 19;
Copper Kettles, page 78*

KEYS

Bronze keys have survived from Roman
times, although most frequently
encountered are those produced from the
17th century onwards of brass, iron and
steel. The designs for these vary greatly,
with prices equally diverse and dependent
largely on the pattern and age of the
piece. A plain 19th-century key (about 4
inches long), for example, with a
minimally decorated loop and notched

hollow shank costs about £5. In contrast, a steel key of the 18th century with fluted shank and scrolled loop may be priced as much as £50, and a late Gothic specimen in excess of £750. Keys of ornate design appeal to collectors of decorative metalwork, but for beginners a range of simple pieces of 18th- and 19th-century origin can be purchased for under £30 at antique fairs and markets. Iron keys are prone to rust, but as long as this has not pitted the metal, the surface can be cleaned satisfactorily.

There are two points of interest in the design of keys: the loop or 'bow' by which it is held; and the 'bit' which engages the lock. The latter can appear of solid or pierced form, and if elaborately notched the value increases. Sometimes it can be shaped like a spade, with geometric notches. The loop comprises a simple oval or ring, sometimes with a heart-shaped inner rim. Pierced and scrolled bows, or those with an insignia such as a coat of arms, are highly collectable.

Padlocks have survived in fewer numbers. A small brass example of Victorian design, complete with key, costs as little as £12–£15. Heavier iron and brass padlocks are priced from about £25 upwards, while unusual iron padlocks of 17th-century manufacture — with extravagant etched strapwork decorations, or incised with heraldic devices — can fetch over £2000 at auction. Examples are included in sales devoted to metalwork or works of art — but for the collector of modest means, country auctions and jumble sales are useful sources, where keys and locks may be found for a few pounds.

For further reading, the following books are recommended: *Locks and Keys throughout the Ages* by Vincent Eras; and *Keys, Their History and Collection* by Eric Monk.

A selection of spade keys from the mid-18th to 19th century. About £15 each

Pair of Staffordshire knife rests in blue and white. £15

Two goosewing knitting sheaths. Left: £28. Right: £22

KNIFE RESTS

These were used to support carving knives on the dinner table, and were usually of dumb-bell shape. They were made in pairs in silver, silver-plate, glass, and porcelain.

Silver examples cost about £40 upwards, but pairs of plated knife rests can be found for as little as £15 in good condition.

Glass rests were made with faceted knob ends, and should be examined carefully for any chips or minor damage. If perfect, they sell for about £15 the pair. Ceramic knife rests are less common, usually designed with silver or plated end pieces, with only the central bar of china or porcelain. These generally range in price from £25–£30.

KNITTING SHEATHS & CASES

Most of the knitting sheaths found for purchase today are of mid-Victorian manufacture, with the 'goose-wing' shape most prevalent.

The sheaths were an aid to knitting, since the needle could be fitted into a hole at the turned end and then tucked into the belt or apron strings. This arrangement supported the needle and left the knitter's hand free to deal with the wool.

Some sheaths were heavily carved in the manner of Welsh love spoons (see: *Love Spoons*), and were probably gifts from sweethearts. Goose-wing sheaths, however, are mostly plain, indicating that they were intended for use rather than ornament. They will cost from about £20, depending on condition. Due to frequent usage, some pieces have weakened at the hole so these have been lined with metal. Check for any splitting of the wood.

'S'-shaped sheaths, and those of scroll or fiddle form, were all produced. Some types resembled paper knives. The sheaths were carved with a variety of stereotyped motifs: crosses, anchors and fish, birds and cockerels, hearts, flowers, and geometric patterns were popular.

LACE

Two major techniques were employed in lace making: needle lace, which is based on embroidery techniques; and bobbin lace, a derivative of weaving.

Needlepoint lace can be recognised by the buttonhole stitches in the composition, whereas bobbin lace has twisted or plaited stitches resembling weaving. There are many forms of lace, the most famous coming from Belgium (point de gaz), Italy (rose point and Burano lace), and Ireland (Youghal). Famous bobbin lace centres included Brussels and Bruges in Belgium, Chantilly in France, and Honiton and the East Midlands where 'Maltese' lace was produced in the second half of the 19th century.

Machine-made lace and net was introduced in the late 1800s. This was often worked on later by hand. Tambour work came from Limerick, Coggleshall and Belgium and consisted of chain stitching worked on net with a tambour hook and frame. Needle-run or Limerick lace used a running or darning stitch technique, while in muslin appliqué cloth shapes were sewn on the net in chain stitch or by couching, known as Carrickmacross lace. Tape lace used machine tapes stitched on to the net in the form of leaves or flowers, of which

Three lace collars. From the top: tape lace, Edwardian lace, and Irish crochet. Prices £10, £18 and £8 respectively

only the very finely executed pieces are of interest to collectors.

Machine-made lace is more evenly textured than handmade lace, and is cheaper to buy. Many lace collars of late 19th-century origin can be found from £10–£20 including examples of Honiton manufacture, Brussels *point de gaz*, and Bedfordshire collar and cuff sets. A large number of pieces are purchased to be worn, and are re-sewn onto dresses and blouses. As a result, lace collars are priced according to their 'wearability' and condition. Examples displaying exquisite detailing, free from tears and mould stains, command the highest prices, from £50 upwards.

Named bobbins from the 18th century. £22 each

19th-century lace-making bobbins made in bone with coloured glass beads. From £15 each

LACE-MAKING BOBBINS

Bobbin lace is made by pinning the previously pricked paper pattern on to a large, firm pillow. The lace thread is then wound around these pins by using a series of bobbins in pairs, and the pattern is gradually woven to make a solid piece of work. For complicated patterns, even on small items such as a baby's christening bonnet, up to 400 bobbins could be used.

The bobbins were made of bone, ivory or wood, and many had coloured glass beads or spangles on the end. The principal use of the spangles was to add extra weight and keep the bobbin steady against the pillow, and they would be mounted on tiny brass or copper wire rings in groups of three to seven. The bobbins themselves would often be intricately carved and would sometimes bear inscriptions, such as 'Love the Giver', or 'Forget Me Not'. One can assume that carved examples with inscriptions were given by a man to his sweetheart, as the name of Joseph or Charles, for example, can be found. These carved bobbins are between £10 and £15 each. Plain, wooden examples (known as 'old maid') will cost about £3 each, and without spangles from about £1.50.

LADLES

These were once part of a dinner set and would be included with the variously sized tureens. They are now collectable in their own right, and can be found at most antique fairs. Their size depends on that of the tureen they served, but usually the ladles are about 8 inches in length. Very rarely were they plain, although the bowl can be undecorated with the ornamentation all on the handle. Flower patterns are popular, as are blue and white examples (see: *Blue and White*

A pottery ladle decorated in blue and white costing about £30

Transfer Printed Ware). They are seldom marked with the maker's mark or backstamp and the only hope of identification is to be lucky enough to come across an example of the dinnerware.

Prices start at about £15 for a fairly plain example; a large ladle with a scenic pattern in blue and white, and in good condition, can cost about £40 upwards.

LAVATORY CHAIN PULLS

Wooden lavatory chain pull with clear message. £15

These exist in astonishing variety, but they do need searching for at antique fairs. Wooden handles, plainly turned and with no inscription will cost about £8–£10, but those made in ceramic will be dearer and will start at about £15.

The ceramic pulls often bore inscriptions such as 'Pull and let go' in black and white, but sometimes the name of the owner of the property was printed on. These are highly collectable and will cost about £10 or more. Occasionally the chain itself can be found with the pull, but one is seldom lucky enough to find these examples.

LEAD FIGURES & ANIMALS

The name to look out for here is Britain, who was the principal maker of lead toys, and one will find the name stamped underneath the figure. Another name to seek is Johillco.

Figures include tradesmen, as well as the ordinary man, woman and child found, for example, in farm sets. Look out for the blacksmith and his anvil, a man with a ladder, the dairyman with his yoke and pails. Railway staff, train passengers and line workers are also collectable, as are policemen. The figures will sell from about £8–£10 upwards, but much depends on the condition and the paintwork.

Animals were made for farm and zoo sets and will include cows, horses and sheep; giraffes, elephants, tigers and so on. Unusual items such as a cat with its litter of kittens will be highly prized by collectors and therefore fetch higher prices. Oddly enough, zoos are less popular with collectors at present.

It is possible to build up complete sets of farms and zoos, and the accessories are available to do this. Trees and fences can be bought for farms, as can cages for zoos. These are usually in metal, not lead, and care must be taken that they are in the correct scale for the figures.

Look out, too, for circus figures, cowboys by Timpo and horse riders by Britain. These are still cheap at between £5–£20.

Selection of lead figures and animals costing from £4 for an animal, £8 each for people

LEAD SOLDIERS

Examples of single figures costing from about £4

As with lead figures and animals (see previous pages), the company named Britain led the field. Single military figures will cost from about £5, but sets and boxed sets will be considerably more. A set of eight figures from the Collector series, for example, will cost from £40 upwards.

Solid lead figures originated in Germany. Britain invented the hollow cast technique, but this can make the figures brittle and prone to damage. Arms and legs go missing, and guns are often broken off. Oval bases indicate that the figures are early, as do the presence of paper labels, and the original box will add considerably to the value of lead soldiers, or sets of soldiers.

All sections of the military were covered, from the Sudanese infantry (about £80 for a set of 19), to the Queen's Own Royal Kent Regiment (about £40 for the set); from the United States Marines (about £80 for a set of 16) to the Sikh Frontier Force Regiment (£70 for a set of 16).

Transport is also included, such as tanks, field guns, lorries and aircraft, but these are near the £100 mark and so can prove prohibitive for the beginner — but well worth looking out for at jumble sales and flea markets, and especially so if they are stamped Britain.

LINEN

Tablecloths, duchess sets for the dressing table, tray cloths, pillow and nightdress cases come under this classification. All are collectable, although at the moment there seems little trade in anything but tablecloths, so perhaps it is a good time to buy.

Many white cotton items are edged with crocheted lace. This can either be of a thick cotton thread or a thinner, more silky fibre. The lace edging is anything from one to 5 inches in depth. Sometimes it will have a shell-shaped finishing edge, sometimes deep points or Vs. Always check this edge for ravelling or loose threads.

The main body of a tablecloth, for example, will sometimes be plain, or will have inserts of matching or constrasting lace. It is important to check these inserts, for all too often the point of an iron will have caught and torn the crochet work.

Some cloths will be embellished with drawn thread work. This is where occasional threads are pulled out of the fabric in sections to make a pattern. The remaining threads are then 'tied' to make the pattern more interesting. Cutwork decorations are where the pattern is

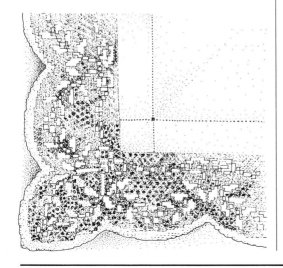

White cotton cloth with deep crochet edging, measuring about 42 inches square. £20–£25

L

literally cut out of, or into, the cloth, the raw edges then being finished off by very fine stitching (see: *Lace*).

Coloured embroidery and cloths are not so desirable. Check for staining; rust marks are there for good and no amount of bleaching will remove them. Also check carefully for darns; these can be done extremely finely.

An afternoon cloth with a reasonable amount of lace trim will cost from about £15–£20; a larger cloth about £30.

LOVE SPOONS

Early 18th-century love spoons will cost over £150, and finding examples of these might deter the beginner, but Welsh love spoons can be found for a much more reasonable price if of a later date. The spoons were carved by young Welshmen as a betrothal gift for their sweethearts and would apparently be for ornament only, as some of the handles can be up to 6 inches across, making them difficult to put to use. Various woods were employed, namely sycamore, fruitwood, yew, beechwood, holly, elm or oak.

The spoons were carved from a single piece of wood, and the graining was important, often being incorporated into

A fine selection of Welsh love spoons showing the varied patterns and shapes that were carved. £30 upwards

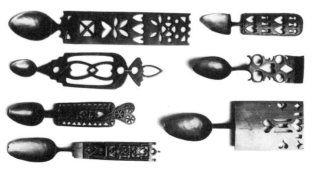

the pattern. Hearts were much used, either standing out in relief or featuring as cut outs at the top of the handle. Ships featured, presumably indicating the couple embarking on the voyage of life together. Less romantically, the ball and chain appeared, symbolic of being tied down! Flowers, animals, and the cornucopia or horn of plenty were also carved, as was the wheel, its spokes indicating a long life. Geometric patterns were popular, as were stencil-like cut outs. A boxwood spoon from Caernarfon in North Wales is in an 'S' shape with no carving at all, relying on the simplicity of its design for its appeal. Simple examples with minimal carving will cost from about £20 or £30, but intricately carved spoons will be about £50 upwards.

Rare finds are those with a double bowl, but these would cost well over a hundred pounds.

LUSTRE WARE

Early English lustre was intended to resemble metal. Platinum or gold was dissolved in strong acid, and various chemicals added. If gold was used but applied thinly on to a dark surface, a copper lustre effect would be achieved; applied thickly, and gold lustre was the result. When painted on white, the resulting colour would be dark pink or pale violet, such as the well-known Sunderland lustre items. Welsh lustre was of the pink variety, and made by the Swansea and Nantgarw factories. It is known as Gaudy Welsh or Gaudy Lustre.

The Sunderland lustre is a generic term for items produced by various factories in the area, although Dixon, Austin and Company made a great deal. Ware commemorating the opening of

Staffordshire cream and sugar set in silver lustre circa 1920. £15–£20 the pair

M

bridges and other historic events was popular, as were names, ships and portraits of celebrities.

Wedgwood lustre was mottled pink with applied orange splashes, known as 'moonlight' or pink splashed with gold, purple or ruby. The Wedgwood lustre is highly prized and out of reach of the ordinary collector. A Gaudy Welsh jug about 5 inches high will cost about £80, a Sunderland jug of a similar size will cost about £100, while an unmarked jug will cost around £80 upwards.

Lustre experienced a revival in the 1920s, when pottery was glazed with an iridescent rainbow sheen. These pieces were made by Grimwades, Crown Devon, Carlton, Kensington and, most well known, Maling. The ground colours used were pastel and delicate: pale green, yellow, cream or blue or pink, sometimes with deep orange as an inner colour, although Carlton produced a deep dark blue, and a dark red known as Rouge Royale.

Prices for Maling lustre depend on the size of the article. A small sweetmeat dish will cost about £10–£12, a large vase with an unusual pattern of willow fronds on white will cost about £50. Kensington lustre is under-rated and a 10-inch vase will cost about £12. A Grimwades fruit bowl in pale blue with a rich orange interior will cost about £15.

MANTEL & SHELF CLOCKS

There is enormous variety in these, but a start for the collector would be the Westminster chiming clock which is just beginning to become collectable. This was made in the 1930s and is recognizable by its musical chime. Sometimes it is found in a long 'Napoleon Hat' style case, but it can be found in other shapes too. The Whittington clock is also collectable. The chime is rather more complicated. Sometimes a clock will have both Westminster and Whittington chimes and these will usually cost more. A simple Westminster finely cased in mahogany will cost about £30–£40, but examples in dark polished oak will often be on sale for about £10. Check that the silvered dial is not scratched or flaked.

Edwardian clocks in mahogany with inlaid shell motifs or banding are also collectable, and a chiming mantel clock in an inverted U shape will cost from £30. Small Napoleon hat shaped clocks no more than about 5 inches high, non-striking will cost about £15, more if the case is in excellent condition.

Gothic clocks are tall, the case sharply angled and coming to a point, twin spires each side, with a glass door reminiscent of a cottage or ogee clock (see: *American Ogee Clocks* and *Cottage Clocks*). These are American and start at about £65. German imitations can be found for the same price.

Clocks made in the 1930s imitating the Jacobean style are chiming clocks and have silver anodized dials, sometimes heavily figured. The chimes can be made silent by the adjustment of a lever. They are still under-rated and can be found for under £30.

Art Deco style mantel clock with anodized dial circa 1935. £20

MARBLE CLOCKS

Despite being called marble clocks, these Victorian clocks are in fact made of Belgian slate. They are extremely heavy as the panels of slate were fixed by cement to a cement base and held in place by metal rods.

The movements were usually of

A very large handsome clock with ornate brass decoration and granite banding to the base.
£100

Smaller marble clock of unusual design, again with brass decoration.
£50–£60

French manufacture and were of high quality. A bell strike or count wheel is earlier than a rack strike or a gong. The pendulum was measured in French inches (just under 1.1 English inches), and was matched to the movement. The serial number of the clock was stamped on to both movement and pendulum. Makers to look out for are Japy Frères, F. Marti, S. Marti, and A. Moughin.

White alabaster was sometimes used for the cases although they were usually black. Decoration would be added in the form of ornate brass mouldings such as winged cherubs, female faces, shell and leaf motifs, and scrollwork. The slate would also be engraved in leaf and flower patterns, curved lines and scrolls. These were then gilded to stand out in contrast to the polished slate. Coloured marble insets were also used and these could be red, green, golden brown, rust and grey.

Clocks varied in size and shape, the smallest being some 6 inches high, the largest about 20 inches by 28 inches. The cases could be oblong and simple, have a brass decorated urn on top, or be of the classical Greek temple shape with varying numbers of pillars each side. The pillars are usually painted black, but can be found in brass. Prices range between about £45–£60 for a Greek temple style clock of moderate size, to £100–£120 for a large clock decorated with malachite and gilding and having a visible escapement.

Some clocks came with garnitures, or side ornaments. These would be urn-shaped, or like pedestals with recessed tops. A garniture will add value to the clock and one can expect to pay about £120 for a medium sized clock with matching garnitures.

Check the clock for chips which can be almost unnoticeable on the black slate, and easily missed. Check too that the pendulum is original (see above). Always lift a marble clock from the base. The cement is old and can come unstuck.

MARY GREGORY GLASS

The name Mary Gregory is used to describe clear or coloured glass items of late 19th century manufacture which have been decorated with white enamelled figures of children. Dressed in typical Victorian style — the boys in knickerbockers, the girls in full-skirted dresses — the figures were placed invariably on a white ground, usually with grass or foliage around them.

It is sometimes thought that the term derived from the American glass decorator, Mary Gregory, who is recorded to have worked at the Boston and Sandwich Glass Company in Massachusetts from 1886 to 1888. The large amount of Mary Gregory glass on the market today, however, would suggest that it could not have been decorated by one person alone. It is more likely that this distinctive style originated

Pair of small beakers in Mary Gregory glass, circa 1880. £60 the pair

in Bohemia (where pieces are still being produced today, and marked as such), and later transferred to factories in England and America. The connection with Mary Gregory remains undocumented, and hence unresolved.

The quality of the enamelling varies considerably, from the finely executed, gleaming white pieces of Bohemian origin, to the flesh-tinted sloppy portrayals created by some English factories. Modern reproductions recall little of the exquisite enamelling found on their Bohemian prototypes, and the children appear chubbier and less attractive.

Mary Gregory glass can be found in a variety of colours: deep blue, dark green and cranberry were popular (see: *Cranberry Glass*), and, more rarely, amber and a paler green were employed.

Prices vary from about £20 for a small cranberry vase, to £40 or £50 for a cranberry jug. A pair of dark blue vases, with a boy on one and a girl on the other, costs about £70. Minor chips will reduce the price considerably, as will poorly enamelled subjects and those in flesh-coloured tints.

MASON'S IRONSTONE

This heavy earthenware first appeared in 1813 when Charles James Mason took out a patent for its manufacture. The new Ironstone was extremely durable and was used for an amazing variety of wares, from dinnerware and miniature vases to vases as large as 5 feet tall, and even fireplaces. The most recognisable colours are the dark blue and vivid orange ornamented with gilding of the 'Japan' pattern, and a small jug about 3 or 4 inches high will cost about £45; a 6 or 7 inch jug will cost nearer £90. Other patterns include willow and Chinese dragon.

The backstamp shows the name 'Masons' above a crown, with 'Patent Ironstone' underneath, or the words 'Fenton Stone Works' enclosed within a rectangle.

In 1848 Charles Mason became bankrupt and the mould and patterns were bought by Francis Morely, later passing to G. L. Ashworth. Mason's Ironstone is being reproduced today and can be bought in department stores, so care must be taken to check the backstamp on pieces seen at antique fairs.

The base of a tureen, showing the early Mason's mark

MATCH HOLDERS & STRIKERS

A Noritaké matchholder with hand-painted design. £18–£20

M atches were invented in 1826, and phosphorus was used as an igniting agent in about 1830. The phosphorus made the matches unstable and so they were contained in metal holders. These were frequently ornamental, with roughened patches for striking. Later examples were made in glass or china, and these have become very collectable.

Glass holders are usually round in shape, in threaded glass with a silver or plated rim. Ceramic holders and strikers were made in a great variety of shapes and designs. Royal Doulton examples are sometimes globular with a roughened surface for striking.

Small bisque figures were made in Victorian times with the holder to the rear of the figure, frequently disguised as a tree trunk, the ribbing on the bark acting as the striker. These will cost from about £12–£15. An amusing match holder uses the lady's fan as a striker. Some holders are simple oblong containers to hold a match box, the aperture at the side revealing the striking part of the box, and these sell for about £12–£15.

M

MAUCHLINE WARE

This wooden souvenir ware was made in the Scottish town of Mauchline from the early 1800s until the 1930s. The small items, made of sycamore, would be decorated by drawing the picture then coating it heavily with varnish for protection. They were scenic and at first were pen and ink sketches, but this gave way to transfer printing in the 1830s. A great many views connected with famous Scottish personalities were produced, such as the Burns' Monument, and Sir Walter Scott's monument, as well as Scottish scenes. English and Welsh holiday resorts were depicted. For example, Llandudno in Wales, Ramsgate, Hastings and Skegness in England. A box which opens out into a watch stand (see: *Watch Stands*) with the transfer picture of Great Yarmouth recently sold for £30.

In about 1860, the use of transfers gave way to photographic scenes being applied to the ware, and these provide a source of interest for the historian. A view of Ventnor in the Isle of Wight shows quite clearly the bathing machines that stood just below the promenade.

A great many articles were made, such

Several small Mauchline ware items priced between about £20 for the pin cushion to £65 for the unusual money box of barrel shape

as snuff boxes, napkin rings, egg cups, and so on.

Check that the picture or scene is well defined and not too rubbed, and that the item itself is in good condition. A small pill box will cost about £15, and napkin ring about £10–£12, a larger item with more than one scene, for example a picture frame with a different scene at each corner, will cost about £40 upwards in good condition.

MONEY BOXES

V ictorian examples were made in wood, metal and pottery. The latter are scarce, and prices will be accordingly higher. Wooden money boxes usually had a 'secret' lid or opening for extracting the money, and these could be either plain or transfer decorated (see: *Mauchline Ware*). The shapes could resemble castles, brass bound caskets, barrels or books as well as being simple oblong boxes. Prices start at around £10.

Tin plate boxes were popular in the 1930s, and the familiar scarlet-pillar box about 6 inches high will cost £30–£35. One shaped like a safe, smaller but with a musical movement, will be £35–£40.

Metal money boxes were usually made of brass or cast iron. A cast iron negro's head with extended hand to put the coin into the slot — the mouth — painted in bright colours will cost about £50, but there are reproductions of this to be found, so care must be taken. Brass appeared in the shape of bears, boots, barrels and banks and these will be from about £30 upwards, although the American 'Novelty Bank' is catalogued at over £350.

China money boxes which had to be broken into to retrieve the contents

A painted metal money box of the 1920s. Designed to resemble a book (Aladdin), it has the added feature of a lock and key. £25

A rather battered metal money box shaped like a cup and saucer. £15

usually come in the shape of houses. A Staffordshire cottage of simple design will cost about £60, with more ornate and decorative examples reaching the hundreds.

MOORCROFT, WILLIAM

He was born in 1872 and received his training at Wedgwood's before joining the James McIntyre company as a designer of art pottery in 1898. In 1913 he opened his own factory in Burslem. His most famous designs are 'Florian' and 'Aurelian', both of which had ornate Art Nouveau flower designs in trailing slipware. These are highly sought after and prices vary between £70 for a small vase to about £300 for a larger example. Other designs were: Claremont, Toad Stool (rare), Hazeldene, Cornflower and Waratah. The most commonly seen pattern is of poppies on a dark blue ground.

A small Moorcroft posy bowl with stylized flowers in pink on a blue/green ground. £45

The backstamp used was a facsimile painted signature, W. Moorcroft, with the early examples more readily decipherable than that of later ones. The name McIntyre also appears on early pieces. Confusion sometimes arises as Moorcroft's son Walter took over in 1945 and he also signed his work W. Moorcroft. Paper labels marked 'By Appointment to the late Queen Mary' fixed to the base of the article can lead the collector into thinking the item is older, but this paper was used from 1949 until 1973.

Bowls, plates, tobacco jars, covered or lidded boxes, clock cases, and vases were all made, and all are highly collectable, with prices rising appreciably.

MOTTO WARE

This is Devon pottery (see: *Torquay and Devon Pottery*) made as souvenir ware and bearing incised messages. Most of the items are domestic, such as teapot stands, cream jugs and sugar basins, marmalade jars and jam pots, sugar casters and small plates.

The ware is usually of a creamy colour with the message in brown lettering. Proverbs, maxims, exhortations and sayings in Devon dialect were all used. For example, a small lidded saucepan reads 'A saucepan though I be, the fire's not meant for me. And as I'm no use as I am, you'd better fill me up with jam'. Other messages read: 'Daun'ee be afraid o' nowt'; 'Guard well thy thoughts. Our thoughts are heard in Heaven'. A cream jug bears the succinct instruction to 'Be canny wi' th' cream' while a proverb tells us 'A stitch in time saves nine'.

Prices at the moment are modest and vary between £4 for a small cream jug, to £8 for the lidded saucepan.

Some collectors aim for specific patterns, such as the black cockerel made mainly by Longpark, but also by

Small lidded saucepan and plate bearing messages. £4–£7

Watcombe and Torquay, or a pattern of leaf-like scrolls by Aller Vale. Other patterns show cottages, sailing boats, and brown and coloured cockerels. Many potteries copied each other, and occasionally one sees a pattern repeated when a designer left one factory to go to another in the area. For example, Charles Collard, one of the best designers, worked at both Aller Vale and Longpark.

MOUSTACHE CUPS & SHAVING MUGS

M oustache cups are large, over-sized cups with a narrow bar just inside the lip on the drinking side. This was to prevent the gentleman's moustache from becoming too wet when he sipped his tea. Despite the fact that the cups are for wholly masculine use, the patterns are, more often than not, floral and feminine, and the cups usually made of a reasonably fine china. The average price is around £20, although searching will find some for between £12 and £15.

Shaving mugs are also for sole male use. These have a shallow perforated top where the soap would be kept, the unwanted water draining through the holes, and an aperture next to this where the shaving brush could be dipped into the hot water. These are also floral decorated as well as plain, and will cost in the region of £15 upwards, depending on the pattern.

Both types can be found with commemorative designs on, and these are more collectable. Prices will vary according to which event is being commemorated (see: *Commemorative Ware*), but generally they start from around £25–£30.

A souvenir pottery shaving mug in plain white. £15

A late 19th-century German moustache cup in painted porcelain. £20

NAILSEA GLASS

Nailsea glass walking stick in blue and white glass. It has some damage to the base, hence only £35

The Nailsea factory was near Bristol and produced various items in dark green or brown glass. They also produced glass with a latticino pattern, loops and swirls (see: *Paperweights*) and the term Nailsea is now descriptive of this type of glass regardless of where it was produced. A great many factories in the Midlands, particularly Stourbridge, copied the designs and were highly successful.

One of the most well-known pieces is the bellows-shaped flask which can be found with pink and white or blue and white loops, although Richardson's made a brandy flask in a combination of red, white and blue, and red, white and green. Although often seen in illustrations, it is rare to see the bellows flask on sale, and it is catalogued at between £250 and £300 for a specimen about 15 inches high.

The Nailsea pattern was used on all manner of novelties from long glass pipes to bells, walking sticks to rolling pins. If damage occurs, pieces can be bought

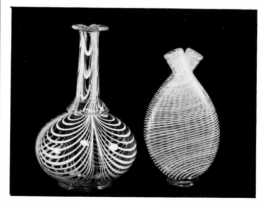

Left: A Nailsea decanter with white loops and whorls. £75
Right: A double flask with opaque stripes. £90

more cheaply, and a bargain was found recently when a rolling pin with pink loops, the knob missing from one end (which does not show when carefully displayed), was purchased for only £10.

NAME BROOCHES

These were made in silver, jet, mother-of-pearl with gold or silver wire applied names, or carved ivory. But the ones seen most often at antique fairs are silver and these would appear to be the most collectable.

They were made either as bar brooches or as round ones. For some reason, the latter are seldom hallmarked, unlike bar brooches. Decorations, in addition to the name, include bluebirds, ivy leaves, hearts, anchors, and forget-me-nots.

The names are Victorian sounding, such as Annie, Agnes or Aggie, Maude, Emma, Edith, Fanny and so on, although more fashionable names such as Stella, Sarah and Madeline can be found, and these look just as attractive when worn with modern clothing. 'Baby' and 'Grannie' brooches were made too.

The brooches make ideal christening gifts, or attractive and personal Christmas and birthday presents.

Name brooches were made from about 1880 until the early 1920s. A silver bar brooch will cost from about £15–£18, the round examples about £5 more as they are hallmarked.

Mother-of-pearl bar brooches are smaller with the name written in gold or silver wire, and these will cost about £12–£15.

Jet name brooches (see: *Jet Jewellery*) will cost about £15, depending on size and complexity of carving and design.

Ornate Victorian brooch in silver. £25

NORITAKÉ CHINA

The Noritaké factory in Japan began production in the late 1890s. They made extremely fine porcelain items such as tea and coffee sets, vases and bowls, and later, novelties such as match box holders, ashtrays and miniature vases, and (not often seen) washstand sets consisting of a large jug and basin, toothbrush holder and soap dish *etc.*

The principal export market was America and the Morimura Brothers were the main importers. Noritaké was also given away as a premium with the bulk purchase of soap by Larkin and Company in the 1930s or could be purchased under a mail order scheme. The majority of Noritaké to be found at antique fairs dates from this period.

The backstamp shows a spider-like symbol within a circle (the Komaru) with the word Noritaké above. The other main backstamp has the word Noritaké above a laurel wreath enclosing the letter M (for Morimura Brothers). All Noritaké ware was marked, and the word Nippon, meaning Japan, does not mean that the item is Noritaké. Backstamp colours are pale blue, green or red. It is difficult to date: the company kept few records, and many were destroyed during the war.

There is a large range of styles, from the scenic patterns in soft yellow, amber and brown showing a house, lake or swan, to the desert scene pattern which shows a man on a camel, with a tent and a fire near by, having a wide border of dark blue and gilding. There are several imitators of this pattern, so always look for the backstamp.

Other patterns include elaborately gilded and ornate designs incorporating flowers, pagodas or idyllic scenes encrusted with gold beading and

A dark red two-handled vase with ornate gilding and hand-painted scene. £50

sometimes banded with colour. A pair of
ornate vases with this gilding in good
condition, of about 6 inches high will cost
about £60. It is important to check the
state of the gilding as it easily becomes
rubbed and worn, and this can devalue
the piece.

Miniature scenic vases without gilding,
in amber tones and standing about 3
inches high will cost about £20. Single
coffee cups and saucers of the demi-tasse
(half-cup) size (see: *Coffee Cans*) will
be between £15 and £25 each. Hatpin
holders are about £15, and small ashtrays
cost £3–£5.

Art Deco pieces of Noritaké are rare
and highly collectable. A pair of vases in
dark brown with a geometric pattern in
vivid colours will cost about £60 (height
about 5 inches). Demi-tasse sets of coffee
pot, cream and sugar, and four cups and
saucers will be between £80 and £150
depending on design, complexity of
pattern and gilding.

*A hand-painted vase
circa 1930, the
colourful painting on a
yellow background. £40*

NUTCRACKERS

These come in two types: those
operating on the screw principle
where the nut is held in an aperture and a
screw is turned to break the nut under
pressure, or — and more common — the
jaw type which operates on the pivot
principle when pressure is applied to the
handles.

Nutcrackers were made in wood or
metal, and screw examples can be found
as round rings (price about £10) or with
the ring ornamented by a gripping hand,
and a long handle operating the screw
(about £80). Wooden nutcrackers were
made in yew, walnut, boxwood, or
fruitwood.

Metal nutcrackers were made in a

*Brass nutcrackers
depicting the
Lincolnshire imp — a
good luck sign — circa
1890. £18*

Crocodile nutcracker in cast iron with hinged jaw. £14

variety of novelty shapes as well as the more prosaic lever form. One can find crocodiles with wide opening jaws, dogs where the tail operates the hinged jaws, figures and faces. The cast iron dog sells for about £12 and is easily found. Faces are more unusual and will cost around £25–£30. A brass example featuring the Lincolnshire Imp — and looking quite evil despite its reputation for bringing good luck — will cost £15–£20.

OIL LAMPS

A brass oil lamp circa 1900 complete with coloured glass shade. £60

These consist of a base, a bowl which contains the oil, a wick carrier, a long glass chimney, and a globular or frilled shade. The variety comes with the shade and the bowl, and the latter can be of glass or pottery. Pottery examples were decorated with flowers, foliage or game birds, such as pheasants, but care must be taken as these are now being reproduced. Check the glazing — the crazing on reproduction models is too even and symmetrical. Glass bowls can be either clear glass, or coloured in dark blue, red or pink.

The shades offer great variety, and both frilled, open, and round shades were made in glass of various colours, the most sought after being vaseline and cranberry (see: *Cranberry Glass* and *Vaseline Glass*). They could be plain opaque glass with finely etched designs in scrolls, acanthus leaves, and free-form patterns, and the frilling would shade from this plain glass to cranberry or vaseline, deepening in tone at the edges.

Bases were made in brass or cast iron. Check the underside for roughness of the casting. Modern examples are not so well finished.

Prices range from about £20 for a brass based lamp with a plain bowl and shade, to about £100 for a cranberry or vaseline glass example, and a variety of lamps can be found moderately priced between these two ranges.

OPALINE GLASS

This is a semi-opaque, translucent glass which has been given its opacity by the addition of tin oxide or bone-ash to the mix. Many pieces of whitish colour possess a pale milky tone, and resemble the porcelain of the early 19th century with their enamelled and cold-painted decorations. Pastel colours were also produced: pale pink, blue, creamy-beige, yellow, green and mauve. A few special shades were developed for the opaline range, mainly by French factories, such as the so-called *gorge de pigeon* ('pigeons neck', a beautiful translucent greyish-mauve) and *bulles de savon* ('soap bubbles', with its delicate rainbow effect). A wide range of decorative effects was produced in France and England from *c*.1830–70, including vases, lamp bases, baskets, carafes, scent bottles and candlesticks. Examples were also manufactured in the USA by the Boston and Sandwich Glass Co., and in Venice after *c*.1930.

Hand-painted opaline vase in shades of brown, rust and creamy beige on white ground. £18

The pale opaline background was an ideal medium for decoration, and the artist was able to paint most effectively on to it. Often, simple floral motifs and border patterns, or applied glass spirals of a different colour, comprised the central ornamentation, in keeping with the elegant shapes of the vessels. The manufacturer relied on the artist to make the piece attractive to the customer.

Many vases and baskets seen today have floral patterns, sometimes fruit. The flowers can be crudely painted, and look almost blotchy, although fine examples are distinctive for their realistically drawn bouquets and garlands in pale hues.

Apart from cold-painted decoration, enamelling was also employed — sometimes in conjunction with coloured pellets which were added to the surface to pick out the design. Gold and turquoise were popular shades, while red and green pellets gave a jewelled effect, emphasizing the matt finish used with this form of decoration.

Iridescent opal, said by one expert to remind him of pearl button glass, was at its best in Art Nouveau design, decorated with layered threads of clear green glass, although other colours were also used.

Collectors should look for vases with painting in good condition, as wear was frequent and rubbed areas will detract from their appeal and value. A large single vase, probably originally one of a pair, can be bought at auction for around £16–£20. Early decorative pieces, from *c.*1830–60, will cost considerably more, and pairs are usually priced from £60 upwards. Small examples can be purchased from about £12 upwards, again depending on their date of manufacture, and attractiveness of colour and shape. Iridescent opal in the Art Nouveau style is highly collectable and a small vase only 5 inches high can command up to £80.

PAPER KNIVES

Victorian newspapers and books were frequently produced with the leaves and pages uncut, so the need for a paper knife was essential. The large paper knives were used for newspapers, the smaller ones for books and letters. The paper knives had large wide blades with round blunted ends, while the letter openers were more stiletto shaped, narrow and pointed.

There is little variation in the blade, apart from the material used, and this could be silver, steel, tortoiseshell, horn, mother-of-pearl, wood or ivory. Decorations on wood could take the form of mosaic patterns (see: *Tunbridgeware*) or scenic pictures (see: *Mauchline Ware*) and these are highly collectable, costing from about £10–£20.

The handles offer the most variety. Sometimes the handle would be finished with a semi-precious stone such as an amethyst, or shaped like a head, a bird or various animals. *Papier mâché* paper knives were flower painted and sometimes this pattern ran down the blade.

Silver knives had large, heavily embossed handles, the hallmark being hidden in the scrolling or patterned foliage. These will start at about £40. A horn opener will be about £10–£15 upwards, while an ebony handled opener with steel blade will cost only about £10.

Top: A Mauchline Ware paper knife with American transfer. £7

Bottom: A letter opener with amethyst and claw decoration. £35

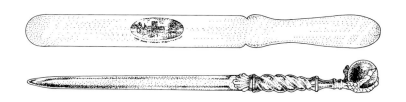

163

PAPERWEIGHTS

Colourful paperweight with spiral twists. £40. Early 20th century

Victorian weight depicting Little Red Riding Hood. £55

Always collectable, paperweights reached their heyday in Victorian times, and enormous numbers were produced from *c.*1845–65. The first glass paperweight was credited to the Venetian glassmaker Pietro Bigaglia, who produced the *millefiori* '(thousand flowers') paperweights. This ornate decoration was made by sandwiching numerous canes of vari-coloured glass together, like a posy, and embedding them in clear, domed glass. French manufacturers designed some of the finest pieces from *c.*1846 onwards, and the factories of Baccarat, Clichy and Saint-Louis excelled in this field.

One of the features of a Baccarat weight was the use of the 'overlay' technique. The paperweight was coated with layers of white or coloured glass and this was then cut away in panels or windows to reveal the pattern inside. Clichy weights can sometimes be identified by the white or pink roses used in the pattern, while Saint-Louis featured coloured canes in wheel formations.

Latticino paperweights have clear and coloured strands of glass criss-crossing to form intricate lacy patterns, while the so-called 'carpet' weights have isolated *millefiori* patterns placed on a plain or latticino background. Cameo or 'sulphide' weights consist of a ceramic medallion set into the clear glass, with portraits, tiny figures, animals and birds in the centre.

In England, paperweights were made as novelties and souvenirs from *c.*1850, although finer pieces were made by the Whitefriars Glass Company, the Birmingham firm of George Bacchus and Sons, and many others.

The Victorians, being avid souvenir collectors, purchased paperweights

Left: Fairly modern Italian weight of millefiori style. £20

Right: Souvenir paperweight with sepia photograph. £12–£15

adorned with places they had been on holiday. Of flattened form, these had a sepia photograph on the base showing tourist sights such as Brighton Pier, or a resort such as Clacton-on-Sea. If the subject is identifiable, the paperweight will cost from £15–£20 upwards, but those with unidentified scenes may be bought for about £8–£10.

Tall, dome-shaped weights intended as door stops can also be found in clear green glass. These Victorian pieces have no pattern other than internal air bubbles which seem to rise and swirl as if from the bottom of the sea. Some feature bubble designs in the form of flowers. Smallish weights will cost about £35, but giant varieties about 5 inches high will cost £60–£80.

Among the best-known modern weights are those made by Paul Ysart, Perthshire Paperweights, and Caithness Glass who produce a large and varied collection each year, sometimes in limited editions. Wedgwood and Whitefriars (now part of Caithness) also manufacture fine paperweights. Perthshire weights are around £40–£60 for a *millefiori* example, and modern Caithness weights start from about £20. Those produced in limited editions can be more expensive.

Another souvenir weight showing a view of the Eiffel Tower. £12

P

PAPIER MACHÉ

The literal meaning of the term *papier mâché* is pulped paper, and this material can prove surprisingly strong when bonded with mastic and pressed into shape. It would then be stoved, rubbed down and smoothed, and finally japanned (a type of lacquer) or varnished. Trays were popular, as well as small tables and cabinets, but these are now very expensive, with a beautifully painted tray about 24 inches across costing well over £200.

A variety of small collectables was made including paper knives, glove boxes and other small boxes, letter holders, trays of about 9 inches in size, photograph frames and small wall shelves.

The base colour is almost always black (red and green are highly prized and rarely seen) and the most common form of decoration is floral. It is important that this painting is not rubbed and that the lacquered surface is not worn or scratched. A glove box some 9 inches by 3 inches will cost about £10 in good condition, a letter holder with more than one section will be about £18–£20.

Mother-of-pearl inlay was also used. Check that this isn't chipped or missing. Examples will cost about £15 for a medium sized box.

Victorian letter rack, attractively patterned. £25

Card box depicting an oriental scene. In good condition £40

Right: Small Vesta case with an attractive illustration. £25

![P]

PARIAN & BISQUE

A small Victorian jug with a good clear design. £25

In the early part of the 19th century marble statues were fashionable, but it was only the rich who could afford the costly portrait busts and figures. The 'poor man's marble' in those days was 'bisque' (or biscuit), an unglazed porcelain or earthenware of chalky appearance. In about 1840, experiments were carried out with the biscuit mixture and a combination of glass and ball clay was added. This produced parian — a milky unglazed porcelain with a slight sheen, translucent when made hollow and held up to the light. Of a finer texture than bisque, parian was ideal for modelling portrait busts and figures displaying notables of the day. Its name derives from its resemblance to the marble found on the island of Paros, off the coast of Greece, where Lord Elgin had found the legendary marbles a few years before.

Parian shrinks during firing, thus giving a clearer definition to the piece as it reduces in size. The high temperatures used in firing vitrify the mix, yielding the smooth surface so typical of parian.

Three manufacturers were involved in the new statuary porcelain: Copeland & Garret, Minton, and T. and R. Boote, although the dispute about who was the first to produce parian has never been settled. Later, firms such as Belleek (see: *Belleek*), W. H. Goss (see: *Crested China*), Robinson and Leadbetter, Wedgwood and Worcester all went into this branch of production, and some fine examples were made. Although Wedgwood's 'Carrara' porcelain is not strictly parian, the formula is so close that it is now categorized as such.

The new medium was used extensively, and busts and allegorical figures were made in their hundreds. But

An attractive pin box about 4 inches in length. Victorian. £35

![P]

☆ **BARGAIN BUY**
A triple spill holder in cream parian found for only £10 due to a minor chip to the base

other items were also made, such as vases, spill holders, tazzas (cake stands), intricately woven baskets, jugs and trinket boxes.

Large figures and busts made by the major manufacturers are expensive for the amateur collector, but small spill vases make an ideal starting point. These are usually unmarked and a small triple owl vase (see illustration) was bought recently for only £15.

Despite the superiority of parian, bisque figures still continued to be made. Because of imperfections left in the finish, these figures were often painted, but left characteristically unglazed. Small figurines of about six inches high can make a charming collection and, with searching, can be found reasonably priced. A small pig, standing on hind legs and holding a pair of cymbals, was found recently for £6, while a boy jockey wearing a white shirt and breeches, with a red, blue and black cap (standing about four inches high) cost only £10.

A figure of a World War One soldier, having a bandaged head and marked 'A Gentleman in Kharki' (*sic*), was priced at only £4 at a car boot sale because of slight damage to the base.

PASTRY CUTTERS

Also known as pastry jiggers or jaggers, the old-fashioned cutter was basically a crimped wheel mounted on a handle of about five or six inches long, which was used in place of a knife for crimping or cutting out a decorative pastry shape. The origins of such jiggers are undocumented, but the Victorians loved gadgets like this, and produced the simple jigger in wood, brass, iron or steel in great numbers. Sometimes a pottery or

168

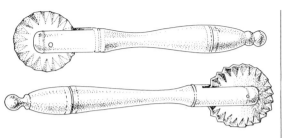

Two Victorian pastry cutters or 'jiggers', made in wood. £8 each

porcelain wheel would be fitted into the wooden handle. Most jiggers have only a wheel at one end, but some can be found with a crimper added at the other end for neatly sealing the edges of a pastie.

Prices are still reasonable, with a simple wooden example costing from around £6 upwards. Examples in silver are much rarer, from about £35 upwards, and can still be used to decorate and trim pastry.

PEARL SHELL WARE

This is the inner shell (or nacre) of the pearl oyster and abalone, which glows with iridescent colour. It was used by the Victorians as decoration and inlay on a great variety of items. The pearl would be split then cut into sections, and would be either used as inlay or to cover the article completely.

Card cases were decorated with squares of pearl set at angles to each other, so producing a shining geometric finish; cotton reel holders had carved mother-of-pearl tops, and buttonhooks had handles carved in feather or candle-end patterns.

Mother-of-pearl was used for buttons, tiny tape measures, small boxes (hinged

Victorian card case in mother-of-pearl, the shell laid in chequer board style. £30

and shaped like mussel shells), pen
knives, fan sticks, etuis, paper knives,
cutlery and sets of nail files and
accessories. Prices range between £5 for a
carved nail file to £15–£20 for a set of
small fruit knives. Check for rubbing or
wear as this will devalue the piece. Game
counters (flat slices of shell either round,
square or fish-shaped) can be found and
cost less than a pound each.

Mother-of-pearl was used a great deal
for inlay, and can be found on *papier
mâché*, wooden boxes and trays, silver
objects, and jet. Prices vary according to
the article, but a *papier mâché* box with
pearl inlay will cost about £18–£25.

PEN KNIVES & FRUIT KNIVES

These date from about 1700 and always
folded for safety while travelling.
They would have silver blades and
straight or pistol grip handles in silver,
mother-of-pearl, horn, ivory, agate or
tortoiseshell. Sometimes the blade was
gilded to protect against the acid in the
fruit. These fruit knives are very
collectable but will cost £80–£100.

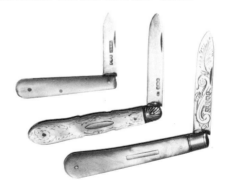

*Three folding fruit
knives made in silver
and mother-of-pearl.
£10–£20*

P

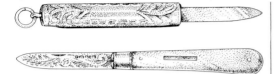

Top: A small silver penknife with steel blade. £18

Bottom: A fruit knife with a mother-of-pearl handle, and ornamented silver blade. £25

Later knives had handles of the same materials but the blades would be of steel and these are cheaper. Mother-of-pearl handles were either plain or carved, or set with inlay silver; silver handles were embossed, engraved, cross-hatched, bright-cut or set with mother-of-pearl. Penknives will start from about £10 for a small lady's version, £15 for a man's, both with silver blades. Check that the blades operate satisfactorily and are not broken, that the spring is good and that the mother-of-pearl (where used) is not chipped or rubbed.

Blades, especially on fruit knives, were also occasionally engraved with a pattern of stars, scrolls, or foliage such as olive branches or vine leaves. Sometimes the owner's name would feature.

PERFUME BOTTLES

These have been made in all shapes, sizes and materials, and range from a superlative example in carved jasper with gold decoration by Fabergé and valued at £4000, to a cut glass decanter-style bottle with faceted stopper from a toilet set, and available for £15.

Glass perfume bottles are an ideal starting point for the beginner and there is a great deal of variety to choose from. Victorian double-ended bottles are very collectable, and these were made in dark jewel colours of red, blue and green, with embossed silver caps. Prices start at about £25. Clear glass bottles were

Art Deco perfume bottle in pale green glass with darker enamelling. £40

Collection of clear glass perfume bottles ranging between £12 and £30

faceted or cut in various patterns, and had hallmarked silver collars. The stopper would be of cut crystal, usually faceted, or the bottles would have a silver cap, plain or embossed. If a cap was used, then a small glass stopper would seal the neck of the bottle. Check that this is in place and not chipped in any way.

Art Deco perfume bottles were made with extravagant tops, and these can be almost as large as the bottle itself. The bottles were angular, the tops round, flat circles of glass set upright in the neck or tall and pointed in triangle or spear shapes. Some were etched with peacocks or other birds; one recently bought has an etching of a boy blowing bubbles on the stopper. Colour, when used, was pale pink, green and blue, and these plainer coloured perfume bottles are relatively cheap and start at about £12.

Commercially produced scent bottles are also collectable, such as the dark blue 'Evening in Paris'. Woolworth's produced a cheap perfume in the 40s. This was sold in a clear glass bottle in the shape of a 'Bonzo' type dog, and this is now collectable and will cost about £10. Scent bottles of a proprietary nature will only be of real value if the label is intact, and if in pristine condition will cost more.

P

PEWTER TANKARDS

These have been used since the 1600s and a rare pear shaped tankard was sold at auction about three years ago for over £5000. But that doesn't mean that reasonably priced tankards cannot be found. Pewter is composed of tin mixed with brass, copper, lead and antimony or bismuth in varying quantities. Early pewter bore touch marks (similar to hallmarks) and the earliest recorded is 1600, the latest 1910.

Victorian tankards are amongst the most affordable, with prices ranging between £10 and £20 for a small pewter measure of about a quarter pint in size. Quart and pint tankards — measures and ale jugs — will cost about £30–£40 for a good example in fine condition, as will the glass-bottomed tankards beloved of the Victorian makers of commemorative items and trophies.

Some tankards bore the owner's name, such as 'Lizzie Smith 1878' which was inscribed in italics on the side of a small tankard — perhaps for gin? — and this was bought for only £8. Very little other decoration was used apart from a series of banding or parallel lines inscribed round the tankard, as it relied on its handle or thumbpiece (if lidded) for decorative attractiveness.

Most had swan neck handles, with ornate thumbpieces such as a bud, heart-and-spray or scroll in tankard shapes such as pear, tulip or spire, but these are generally early specimens.

Never polish an old tankard to a bright finish, as this will destroy the patina and ruin its value. A light dusting with a soft cloth is all that is needed. If very dirty, then the tankard can be washed, using a good quality washing up liquid. Rinse thoroughly then polish lightly.

Pewter tankards such as this can be bought for about £30

P

PHOTOGRAPH ALBUMS

The finest of these are Victorian. They vary in size from about 4 by 6 inch books, to large albums of about 9 by 12 inches. The smaller books are plain, with square or oval cut outs into which to insert the photograph. The larger albums gave more scope for decoration, and they can be found beautifully decorated. Alternate pages would be plain, with perhaps room to insert four or more photographs, while the other pages would have room for only one larger picture. This page would be painted, perhaps with flowers and leaves and daffodils; iris, primroses and bluebells, roses and ferns were all popular. Sometimes the painting would take the form of a scene, rolling hills and woodland maybe, all tastefully framing the oval or square photo.

The decorated albums cost more and a typical example will cost between £20 and £40. It is important to check that the cut out sections are not torn, and that the

Pages from a Victorian album showing the attractive designs used. £40 in good condition, and with no damage to the oval cutouts

stitching in the spine of the book is tight and secure. Small albums are about £10.

If there are photographs in the album, this will raise the price, especially if the pictures are interesting, perhaps showing the fashion of the time. But one can find bargains — a rather shabby album was recently bought for only £5 and was found to contain some fine examples of Victorian dress and interiors.

Albums were made of leather, fabric, velvet or (rarely) tortoiseshell, and were often embellished with gilt lines and scrolls or inlaid with silver or mother-of-pearl. Some had heavy and ornate brass clasps and these will cost around £50.

PHOTOGRAPHS

The capturing of the photographic image on paper was achieved by W. Fox Talbot in 1834, and photographs have never waned in popularity. Early photographs can be regarded as historical documents, as the fashions and scenes of the time were recorded and ones to look out for are not the ubiquitous cathedrals and main streets (unless showing transport) but the more off-beat snaps of tradesmen plying their craft, children playing, fishermen mending their nets etc.

Military photographs are collectable, especially when related to the Boer War, the Spanish Civil War, and World War I, but these can prove expensive and a single photo from the Crimean War can cost about £50.

Street scenes and landscapes can be bought quite cheaply for anything up to £10. Victorian portraits and family groups are about the same price, as are photographs of foreign scenes and people. Jumble sales are a good place to buy, as old albums are often carelessly discarded.

P

PICKLE DISHES

These are leaf-shaped dishes which were used largely in the 18th and 19th century to display pickles and spices on the meal table. Deeper dishes would have possibly been used to hold the butter.

A surprising number of pickle dishes have survived and almost all are blue and white (see: *Blue and White Transfer Printed Ware*).

Factories such as Worcester, Caughley, Lowestoft, Spode, Wedgwood, Derby and Bow all made the dishes, and with varying distinctive designs. Worcester used a floral and grape vine pattern, Ridgeway's decorated them with typically English scenes from their Oxford and Cambridge College Series, and Caughley used oriental scenes.

There are various shapes within the leaf design, and the dishes were made in graded sizes, presumably to make for easier stacking in storage. Bow produced eight or nine shapes, Worcester had about eight, while Caughley only produced four.

Prices vary between £20 and £60, depending on whether the dish is marked or not.

A blue and white pickle dish in leaf shape. £60

PINCUSHION DOLLS

These are also known as half-dolls and date back to Victorian and Edwardian times, when the dolls were sewn on to hooped covers for disguising all manner of things. Made in pottery or fine porcelain, the dolls measure between one and nine inches. They can look like elegant court ladies, or flappers from the 20s and 30s.

The firm of W. Goebel in Germany made the half-dolls mounted on tea and coffee pot cosies, for use as pincushions, cake covers, and even lampshades. Dressel and Kister made them as pincushions, parasol handles, hatpin holders, as ornaments for powder puffs, nightdress cases and so on.

The dolls are rarely seen with their original bases, other than pincushions, and are bought in their 'undressed' state. They were originally sewn on to the object they decorated, or fixed to a wire cage which was then covered, and one can find a series of small fixing holes at the edge of the china just below the waist. Some dolls would sit on a pincushion, the flounced skirt showing an elegant pair of legs, and these legs are now sold separately. A few rare dolls came equipped with a mohair wig (see illustration) and these will cost £50–£60.

Made mainly in France and Germany, and sometimes marked with their country of origin or maker's name, the dolls are becoming extremely collectable. Many copy the look of Marie Antoinette with a high formal hairstyle, others wear hats reminiscent of Gainsborough or Watteau

A selection of half-dolls ranging in price from £25 for the unclothed court lady to £55 for the example to her right in the mohair wig. The hatted 1930s girl was a bargain at £10 when found at a flea market

P

paintings. Rare examples show dolls in Tyrolean or Welsh costume, or dressed as gypsies. These now cost about £70 each. Pierrot dolls were also made and these cost about £80.

Check for damage — necks are particularly vulnerable. Check the features too. Some dolls are finely made with the facial features well defined; others are less well done and these will be cheaper.

Dolls from the the 1920s and 30s are now highly prized and will cost about £30–£35; more mundane half-dolls will cost £15–£25.

PINCUSHIONS

The Victorians made them in great variety. There were plump velvet hearts, beribboned and decked with lace, or in a patchwork of fabrics decorated with beads and sequins. Some, given as presents to a new mother, came patterned with pins spelling the words 'Spare the Mother' or 'Bless the Babe'. Souvenir pincushions with wooden bases were brought back from holiday (see: *Mauchline Ware* and *Tunbridgeware*). Wooden cushions were also made shaped like caskets, and these were sometimes weighted in order to anchor the material

Left: A basket-shaped pincushion made in ivory. In good condition £35

Right: Shaped like a violin, this velvet pincushion is worn, but still interesting. £15

178

being sewn. The lid would often be made to lift off, providing a storage place for small sewing items.

Metal-based pincushions were made in the form of animals with a padded velvet top. Pigs, donkeys, dogs and birds featured, as did shoes, baskets and cradles. The metal could be base, silver or brass: brass pigs are highly collectable and will cost from £30–£40. Silver pincushions are beyond the reach of the average collector, but continental silver is affordable at about £40–£50.

Tiny round pincushions were made topped with red, blue or green velvet or silk. The base could be carved or pierced ivory, and of a turret shape, or turned wood such as walnut in an egg cup or rounded bucket shape. The latter start at around £20.

Carved wooden pincushion with red velvet pad. £25

Padded cushions came shaped like discs, playing cards, were decorated with shells or embroidered with lines to resemble the spokes of a wheel. More ornate examples had floral patterns worked in beads; sailors' and soldiers' pincushions given as a gift to a loved one had the design picked out in glass headed pins, and sometimes bore the regimental badge in silk. These will cost £60 or more.

PLASTER FIGURES

These are difficult to find undamaged, and many have been re-sprayed or painted in order to hide defects. The most popular at the moment are the figures or figure groups from the 1920s and 30s. Tall girls striding along with windblown hair, one or two dogs on a leash, are typical and these will cost from £40–£70 depending on condition. Dancers are a favourite too and a 1930s couple in

Green plaster nude, one of a pair of bookends. £25–£28 if bought separately, about £60 for the pair

dancing pose can be found for £20 upwards. Beware of those that have a pristine bronze or silver finish; they have more than likely been re-painted and while this does not detract from the attractiveness of the piece, it does devalue it in terms of originality.

Plaster nudes seem to have disappeared from the scene at antique fairs. An extensive range of green painted nudes were made in various poses in the late 1930s but as plaster is very prone to damage, many of these suffered unsightly chips. Those in good condition are between £25 and £35 depending on the interest in the pose.

Children often feature, as do young girls in layered skirted dresses and poke bonnets. The latter are usually in shades of pink and can be found for about £10. A good quality child's head, finely modelled and in good condition (check the nose for chips) will be about £40–£60, possibly more if signed and dated on the back.

Dogs, especially alsatians, were popular, and these can be seen standing or reclining on long bases. Usually made in pairs they will cost about £12 each, £20 for a pair.

PLASTIC

Plastic is a material which, when softened by heat, can be moulded into a required shape, and hold that shape when set. Horn is a natural plastic, as are amber, bone, tortoiseshell and shellac.

The first semi-synthetic plastic was vulcanized rubber, known as 'Vulcanite' and discovered in 1838 by Charles Goodyear. In 1855, 'Parkesine' (named after its English inventor, Alexander Parkes) made its appearance. Objects such as shoe horns, handles, fishing reels and bracelets were manufactured, but the brittleness of the material has made these objects rare today. In 1869 the Hyatt brothers in America produced celluloid (a trade name that is now generic) which was far more durable.

Experiments went on and improved plastics such as Bakelite, Bandalasta, and Linga-Longa were market leaders (see: *Bakelite*). These materials were popular with numerous designers in the 1930s — even René Lalique created plastic accessories — but with the introduction of better injection moulding machines, new light-coloured plastics appeared and gradually superseded older types such as bakelite.

Initially, production concentrated on domestic items such as egg cups, cruets, picnic sets, lampshades and trinket sets. But with the booming beauty business in the early 20th century, companies such as Yardley packaged their cosmetics in the new urea formaldehyde material. Plastic lent itself well to sharp moulding and high relief, and ornate cigarette boxes and compacts were produced, their lids beautifully decorated with classical scenes. Stylish jewellery (often in imitation of other materials such as lapis lazuli, jade, ivory, tortoiseshell and

Selection of items made in various plastics, priced from £5 upwards

amber) was also created, and took many bold and imaginative forms.

Plastics are still being developed, becoming more sophisticated and an indispensable part of our lives. Early plastics are highly collectable, although Victorian celluloid pieces are rare.

PLAYING CARDS

Miniature boxed Patience cards. The box is slightly worn but the cards are in good condition and complete. £5–£8

E arly cards of the 18th century will cost about £50 or £60 a pack, but later packs, especially those of the 20th century, are much cheaper. After about 1850, cards become double-headed; before that the court cards were printed only one way up. Later that century, playing cards lost their square appearance and gained rounded corners.

Cards of the 20th century commemorate all sorts of events, and the 'Victory' pack was brought out at the end of World War II. Advertising featured a great deal and cigarette manufacturers such as Senior Service, Woodbines, and Players produced packs of playing cards. Schweppes brought out a series of Domino cards with an advertisement for their table waters on the back, and these cost about £5.

Girls, especially nudes and pin ups

have been popular for a long time and a 1950s pack showing different nude girls will cost about £3 or £4. The better the quality of the photograph, the dearer the cards.

Card games for children such as Snap, brought out by Cow and Gate (£3–£4) and Happy Families by Chad Valley (£9–£10) are collectable, as are cards featuring Mickey Mouse, and these will cost £10–£12.

Miniature packs of patience cards, sometimes as double packs, encased in red or blue boxes will be about £5, while the word game of Lexicon will be about £4. Double packs of cards from the 1930s showing chocolate box type girls or scenes can cost as little as £3 or £4. Cards with railway scenes are £4–£5.

Tarot cards are much larger than ordinary playing cards and have a variety of colourful and esoteric images on the back. Prices for these start at about £20–£30 and can rise much higher.

Check that the cards are in good condition. The backs should be un-rubbed; the corners not dog-eared or torn. There should be 52 cards in a pack plus two jokers.

Late Victorian game of Snap. £20 in good condition

POOLE POTTERY

The Carter Stabler Adams pottery of Poole is rapidly becoming collectable. It was first made in the 1920s. The red earthenware was covered with a grey-white slip and a semi-matt clear glaze. The painting was applied in soluble colours before firing, thus giving a slightly fuzzy outline to the patterns. Many of the designs were by Truda Carter (formerly Truda Adams) and were free-form flowers, leaves and tendrils, largely based on embroidery patterns, and in soft colours of green, yellow, blue, pink and purple. The back-stamp was an impressed rectangle with 'Carter Stabler Adams. Poole. England' in capital letters inside, or with the words Poole England.

A great many vases, flower holders and fruit bowls were made and these range in price from £10 for a small vase, to £30–£40 for a well decorated fruit bowl.

Also around this time, Poole brought out their studio ware. This was buff coloured stoneware with geometric designs in blue and yellow, and green was also used. The mark reads 'Carter & Co Poole', impressed in script. A medium sized vase will be about £40.

The 1950s saw another type of studio ware and this is in complete contrast, with plates, dishes, vases, bowls and small dishes in trapezoid shapes. The colours used were bright and vivid — red, orange, yellow, and a sharp lime green. Patterns were abstract, or stylized such as a large brown oak leaf against a black background. This ware bears the Dolphin mark in black underglaze printing. Prices are low as yet, although there is a trend towards collecting. A large dished bowl will cost about £20, a small nut dish about £7.

A Carter Stabler Adams vase with typical pattern in soft blues and mauve. £40

PORCELAIN FIGURES

Factories such as Meissen, Dresden, Sèvres, Bow and Chelsea produced figures that are generally too expensive for the average collector, but there are many continental factories that made attractive examples which are not too highly priced. These include figures by Sitzendorf, Höchst, Volkstedt and Berlin.

A Sitzendorf figure group of a man

P

and a girl, he wearing a tricorn hat, breeches, a long coat and waistcoat, she in a panniered dress with sprigging on the underskirt will cost about £60. Sitzendorf specialized in copying Meissen figures, and a single example of their 'Monkey Band' will cost around £25–£35.

It is worth remembering that minor damage such as chips, missing fingers on the hand, or the head having been knocked off and replaced will greatly affect the price, and an attractive collection can be built up quite cheaply if one can ignore these blemishes. A miniature figure cost £15 at auction because of minor damage. A Berlin cherub perched among reeds and bulrushes was bought for only £10 as one of the bulrushes was missing, and a Meissen figure group in blue and white of mother and cherub-like child cost only £20 because of more major damage (but not enough to spoil the charm of the piece).

☆ **BARGAIN BUY**
Sitzendorf figure group. Normally this would cost about £60, but minor chips, and damage to the man's arm where it is hidden behind the girl reduced the cost to £20

POSTCARDS

These have been in existence since 1869 (1870 in Britain) and are the third largest collectable item after stamps and coins. The first postcards issued had the address on one side, the picture and message on the other. But in 1902 the design changed to have the message and the address on the same side.

The most collectable cards were issued from 1900–1914. The standard of design was excellent and covered a wide range of subjects. Look out for cards by Raphael Tuck, especially the 'Empire' and 'oilette' series.

Cards on display at antique fairs are divided into categories such as glamour, comic, railways, transport, actors and

Three collectable postcards. 'Springtime' will cost about £1.50; the romantic couple is also £1.50, and the cartoon type of card is £2.50

actresses, and so on. Geographical cards are usually divided into counties.

Street scenes are collectable, especially those showing the fashions and transport of the day, and whereas a view of Bipsham Church will cost about 50 pence, a view of a street scene showing a horse-drawn tram will cost £20 or more.

Cards showing film stars such as Errol Flynn, Spencer Tracey or Marlene Dietrich will cost between £1.50 and £5. Studies of nudes and bathing beauties (classed as 'glamour') will be between £1 and £8, as are comic cards. Look out for Donald McGill and Tom Brown.

Silk postcards issued during World War I start at about £3, but can cost as much as £30 if showing a picture of a named ship. Louis Wain cards with pictures of cats will cost about £12 (see: *Wain, Louis*). Sets of cards such as the comic series 'How To Manage a Husband' will cost £12–£15 for a set of twelve; 'Pierrot', a set of nine cards by C. W. Faulkener & Co, will cost £35–£40.

POT LIDS

Prices for these have remained fairly stagnant recently, so now might be a good time to start collecting. Pot lids date from around 1845 when transfer printing on china and pottery was made possible (see: *Blue and White Transfer Printed Ware*).

It is possible to recognize early examples as they generally have flat tops with small crazing, and one of the most popular subjects was a view of Pegwell Bay, or a bear motif. Tops then became convex, the crazing larger, and even later examples were heavier in texture, the crazing larger and more uniform. Colours were not so good either. Coloured pot lids were in production for only about 50 years, while monochrome lids were being produced right up until the 1930s.

Food manufacturers used the pots, advertising their wares on the lids. Meat and fish paste lids are prevalent, such as anchovy paste lids made for Crosse and Blackwell, which will cost about £20–£30. Cosmetic manufacturers soon followed suit and one can find lids advertising glycerine cream, shaving cream, and a cure for chapped hands. These are all monochrome.

Coloured lids showed personalities such as the Duke of Wellington, Queen Victoria, Prince Albert, and Garibaldi. Commemorative lids were issued for the wedding of the Prince of Wales to Princess Alexandra. Prices start at about £20–£25 for a lid showing Dr Johnson, to over a hundred pounds for one featuring Queen Victoria and the Prince Consort.

Scenes and views were featured. Shakespeare's birthplace will start at £25–£30, a view of Hong Kong Harbour will cost £35 upwards, and Trafalgar Square costs about the same. Unnamed

A pot lid decorated with black transfer printing.
£15

views and scenes of village life start at about £35, *eg* 'Feeding the Chickens' starts at £45, the 'Faithful Shepherd' is £60–£70, and the 'Old Water Mill' is £40–£55.

Check the lids for chips or damage, also for restoration. Pale colours are not so collectable.

PRESS-MOULDED GLASS

A lso known as pressed glass, these mass-produced wares made their appearance in America in *c.*1827, and shortly afterwards in Britain and Europe. Previously, glass was free-blown or mould-blown, on to which designs could be painted, etched or cut delicately by hand. Press-moulding by machine gave a sharp, crisp finish to the shapes and ornamental surfaces of wares, due to the pressure of the mould, and made it possible for the average householder to have decorative glass on his or her table — resembling the expensive hand-cut pieces supplied to the wealthy.

Pressed glass is identifiable in a number of ways. There are always mould lines to be found, although in many cases — especially ornamental objects — these were polished out and are only faintly visible. The mould lines appear invariably in threes, and divide the object which was made in thirds, unlike cheaper glass which was moulded in half or quarter parts. The pattern is always sharp to the touch and clearly defined. The designs were applied to either the inner or outer surface, and did not necessarily follow the contour of the piece.

One advantage of press-moulding for the collector is that pieces were able to be

Edwardian matchbox holder with seasonal message, made in clear glass. £35

marked by the maker, and if the registered design number is also known, items can be dated accurately — always a difficult task with unmarked glass. This information adds interest to the piece for the collector.

The main manufacturers in England were Sowerby, Davidson, Greener, Derbyshire and Webb. Their pieces were nearly always marked, usually stamped on the bottom of the article with the factory name or symbol. The Sowerby mark shows a peacock's head wearing what appears to be a plume of feathers. Sometimes indistinct, it has also been described as resembling a seal balancing a ball on its head.

The firm of George Davidson used the top half of an heraldic lion rising rampantly from a brick-patterned turret, a mark which should not be confused with that of Henry Greener's factory which consisted similarly of an heraldic lion, but turret-less and holding a five-pointed star. A later Greener mark shows a thinner lion holding what appears to be a long axe. John Derbyshire used an anchor mark with the letters 'JD' across the shaft, while Thomas Webb employed various marks, such as the name Webb in a square within a diamond, or simply the Webb name alone.

Pressed glass was made in many colours and designs (see: *Carnival Glass* and *Vaseline Glass*), but the cheapest, and in some ways, the most interesting pieces are those of clear glass.

A huge amount of tableware was produced in America and Europe from the second quarter of the 19th century, designed to resemble hand-cut glass. Comports and cakestands, fruit and sugar bowls, cream and water jugs are all intricately patterned, and their sharply moulded faceted surfaces catch the light for added sparkle.

Victorian marbled glass spill vase in purple and white (slag glass), bearing the Sowerby trademark. £25

The registered trademarks and design numbers are sometimes difficult to see, in which case it is important to feel the stamps with the fingertips while keeping the eyes shut. In this way, a small raised bump can be felt which, on closer examination, will reveal the sought-after information. Sometimes this appears on the inside of a bowl or vase, and not under the foot.

Commemorative glass (see: *Commemorative Glass*) came into its own with the advent of press-moulding, and numerous historical scenes, events and slogans appeared commonly on plates, butter dishes and sugar bowls. Queen Victoria's Jubilee gave rise to a whole range of designs and inscriptions. Royal weddings, births, marriages and accessions became the subject of many pressed glass wares, and notable statesmen and other personalities of the day were also portrayed.

1930s flower vase in clear pressed glass with holder for stems. £22

Not all items were intended for use, and some amusing novelties were created. Due to the intricacy of the moulds, decorative items such as glass boots and shoes were made with great accuracy, correct in every detail. Examples of black glass are particularly attractive, since their relief surfaces stand out sharply.

Other imaginative pieces included animal and bird figures which were used to adorn Victorian mantelshelves; elephants which carried square salt containers on their backs; swan-shaped spill vases, designed as tables ornaments, and menu holders. The lions at the foot of Nelson's Column, designed by Landseer, were copied faithfully in pressed glass by John Derbyshire's factory and are now much sought after. Some commemorative figures were also made, notably of Queen Victoria, although these are rarely seen for purchase.

Apart from vaseline and carnival

pressed glass, pieces were made in a variety of colours — turquoise and yellow pearline; shades of green and yellow; an opalescent glass of whitish hue, ideal for portraying swans; translucent and opaque shades of amber, black, dark red, or with marbled designs known as slag or 'end-of-day' glass.

Slag glass appears in yellow, red, turquoise, white, green and mauvey purple, often in variegated and marbled combinations. The name slag is derived from the waste slag or scum (skimmed from molten steel) which was deliberately mixed with the glass in its manufacture to achieve the desired streaky effect. The term end-of-day comes from the belief that the glass left over after a day's work was mixed together and then re-used. However, this is unlikely since the furnaces operated 24 hours a day, and the marbling was the result of a carefully worked out formula.

Pressed wares make an ideal starting point for those interested in Victorian glass, and the majority of pieces remain reasonably priced. Indeed, examples of clear pressed glass appear to be ignored and little appreciated, and there is still great scope for collectors in this field to buy cheaply.

Attractive fruit bowls and comports can be purchased for as little as £10, although for marked and finely pressed examples, prices will start from £15. Coloured press glass, and particularly slagware with its marbled patterns, may be priced from £18 upwards for a small square dish.

Pearline pieces cost from around £20–£30 for a small cream and sugar set, and a glass boot or shoe will normally sell for about £25. The latter make attractive mantlepiece ornaments, when aranged in groups, and appeal greatly to collectors of 'Victoriana'.

RADFORD, ELIZABETH

Beige vase with hand-painted flowers in shades of purple and mauve. £15

She worked as a painter and designer for the firm of H. J. Wood in Burslem in the 1930s and the backstamp for 1935 onwards shows a flowing signature, E. Radford, or Elizabeth Radford, England. Hand painted.

The wares are pastel, the decorative colours soft and slightly fuzzy. Anemones painted in tones of purple, mauve and pink are most commonly seen and this pattern was used extensively on vases, cruets, cheese dishes, nut dishes, cream jugs, sugar basins, and so on. A matching pair of cruets will cost about £7, a cream and sugar about £10.

Other patterns include hyacinths and delphiniums in soft blues, meadow flowers in pink and yellow. A small oval dish with a piecrust edge in the latter will cost about £10. A vase with frond-like leaves in dark green will be about £15.

The collecting of Elizabeth Radford ware is still fairly recent and bargains can be found at flea markets and even antique fairs. Prices remain low, but indications are that they will rise rapidly within the next year or so.

RADIOS

Early radios can cost as much as £400–£500 and the collector is advised to look at examples from the 1930s, where prices are more moderate. It was then that the radio became more of a piece of furniture than it had been before, and the cabinets were designed to fit in with the decor. Frank Murphy of Murphy Radios was an innovator and used wooden cabinets veneered in bird's eye maple, walnut and beech. An A24 Murphy Radio will cost about £50–£60 today. Other manufacturers followed suit, and Pye produced their Twintriple Portable made in walnut, which will cost about £60.

Fashion dictated the use of bakelite (see: *Bakelite*) and it was not long before this material was widely used for radio cabinets. The Ekco AD65, first seen in 1934 was circular in shape, with a moulded black bakelite case, chrome plated fittings, and a semi-circular celluloid dial. This has a value of nearly £100 today.

1939 radio by E. K. Cole Ltd with imitation leather covering. £35

Art Deco style radio with bakelite case, made in 1931. £70

RHEAD, CHARLOTTE

She was a pottery designer and painter whose work is now becoming very collectable. Born in 1885, Charlotte Rhead worked at many factories until her death in 1947. The first factory was T. R. Boote who made tiles, followed by Bursley Ltd, the Crown Pottery in Burslem (part of H.J. Wood), Burgess & Leigh (makers of Burleigh ware), A.G. Richardson (makers of Crown Ducal), and later, back at H.J. Wood's factory.

Most of her work bore a backstamp, with the exception of the 'stitchware' pieces which she designed and which were produced in large quantities. The first backstamp shows the name Rhead in capital letters, standing to the right of a capital 'L', the lower arm of which stretched beneath the surname. This was later replaced by a similar backstamp, but using the letter C instead of L, presumably when Charlotte dropped her nickname of Lottie in favour of Charlotte. A facsimile signature was stamped on Wood's ware, sometimes printed in lower case italics.

Her specialization was tube-lining, a form of slipware decoration which looks as if it has been applied with an icing bag. She conformed with other designers of the day in the use of bright colours, abstract and geometric designs, and stylized trees, flowers and foliage. Her later work became more abstract and lighter in tone, such as the 'Florentine' pattern which had a series of geometric curves outlined in black against a background of brown mottling.

The floral patterns used, showed a great delicacy of colour. For example, a large plaque bearing the 'Wistaria' pattern shows a drooping spray of the flowers painted in purple and pink against a creamy background, the rim of the plaque being edged with green. Some of her work showed an Eastern influence, such as 'Byzantine', 'Omar', 'Persian Rose' and 'Manchu' which shows a dragon writhing on a green background beneath cloud-like scrolls.

A small vase about 5 inches high, lightly tube-lined in pastel colours will cost about £30; a large plaque costs between £60 and £100 depending on the pattern and colours. An unsigned 'stitchware' vase will cost only £20.

ROLLING PINS

These were made in glass, china and wood and the latter will frequently be seen at antique fairs. They can be found with short knobbed ends or with long handles that are free-moving, and these

Victorian rolling pin, hand-painted and lacquered. £30

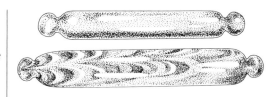

Top: Pale green rolling pin with no decoration. £25. Bottom: Nailsea glass rolling pin in pink and white. £40

will cost from £5. Occasionally one can find rolling pins with interchangeable 'sleeves', one being plain, the other carved in floral or other patterns. This type was used for rolling out shortbread in a decorative design. Prices start at around £15. Scottish oatmeal rollers were carved with deep concentric grooves and an early example will start at about £20–£25.

China rolling pins were intended to keep the pastry cool and many carried advertising slogans or recipes, transfer printed in black and white. These are highly collectable and cost about £40.

Glass rolling pins were ornamental rather than functional and generally took the form of hollow tubes with rounded knob-like ends. They were decorated by loops and swirls of colour in the glass, usually pink and white, or dark blue and white (see: *Nailsea Glass*) and will cost around £40 for a good example.

Royal Doulton figure of Miss Muffet designed by Leslie Harradine. Issued 1940–1967. £70

ROYAL DOULTON FIGURES

The majority of these are well designed girls and women, and they have been made since 1913, since when over 2000 different models have been produced. Many have been withdrawn and, since 1938 this policy of withdrawal has kept the number of figures in circulation down to about 200. Prices vary enormously, but the earlier the figure and its withdrawal, the more it will cost. Each figure is marked with an HN number, the first one being 'Darling' modelled by Charles Vyse and still in production today.

Some male figures were made, such as the 'Jester' (HN1295), withdrawn in 1949 and recently valued at about £300, and 'Sir Walter Raleigh' (HN2015) withdrawn in 1955 and costing over £200 today.

But not all figures are so expensive. 'The Orange Lady' (HN1759) withdrawn in 1979 will be about £80, as will 'Bess' (HN2002) withdrawn in 1969.

Serious collectors will find it useful to have a copy of the book published on Royal Doulton figures, as this gives dates of initial production and the date of withdrawal for each HN number. It is available at bookshops selling books on antiques, and at larger fairs.

SALTS

Victorian salts are among the most collectable. Silver of this era is affordable, unlike earlier examples. The salts would sometimes be gilded to guard against the corrosive action of the salt, especially if shell shaped, or would have a blue glass liner for protection. These small salts will cost about £30–£40.

Salts made in silver plate or pewter could resemble miniature cauldrons, and if the liners for these are missing or broken, there is very little likelihood of replacement. Cost will be about £10 upwards for a pretty example.

Glass salts were made in great variety after the advent of pressed glass (see: *Press Moulded Glass*) and they were available in a variety of colours from red, blue, green, amber, yellow and clear, to marbled colours of green, blue and amethyst. The most frequently seen —

*Top: Transparent pressed glass salt. £12–£15
Bottom: Simply moulded clear glass salt. £3*

and the cheapest — are those in clear glass. They may be round, oval, square or boat-shaped, have flat bases, stand on tiny knobbed feet, or on a single footed stem. They may be plain, ribbed or faceted, and could have star cutting on the base.

Chips are frequent, so check carefully. Prices range between £2 for a tiny round salt in clear glass, to about £10 for a larger example of good design in marbled slag glass.

SAMPLERS

O riginally made as samples of patterns and stitches and kept for reference, the early samplers were long and narrow, sometimes only 6 or 7 inches wide, but as long as 30 inches. It was not·until the mid-1700s that they took on their square shape.

The majority of Victorian samplers were made by young girls in the schoolroom, presumably so that they could learn their embroidery stitches. These usually bore the name of their maker, and were signed and dated. The stitches used were cross stitch, flat, satin, eyelet, tent, running, chain, ladder and fishbone stitch and were worked in silk, fine wool, or linen thread.

An attractive sampler, worked in simple cross stitch. £90

Some simple samplers consist of the alphabet, numbers and a motto or religious text. These were probably school exercises and will cost from about £40. Many samplers had moral or religious themes, and some were worked with verses: 'O Lord I would delight in thee, And on thy care depend. To thee in every trouble flee, My best, my only friend'. The Ten Commandments was also a favourite, often set out in tablet form similar to those seen in churches, and sometimes the Lord's Prayer was worked. Other popular subjects were buildings, houses, windmills, ships, flowers and trees.

Check that the samplers are in good condition, without breaks in the thread or letters missing. Ideally, the colours should be bright and unfaded, and the fabric itself undamaged and not rotten.

SCALES, KITCHEN

Domestic scales fall into two types: the spring balance, and a beam-like scale which uses weights to counterbalance the goods. The spring balance scale is upright on a cast iron or tin plate base, with a round dial marked in ounces and pounds below the cruciform arms which support the pan. Salter made an attractive balance scale in black cast iron with a brass dial. But most dials were of white enamel. Unfortunately many people painted the base to match their kitchen decor, and the beauty of the cast iron is lost.

The pan was a shallow round dish made in base metal, rarely brass, and this type of scale will cost from about £20 for

Cast iron butter scales with ceramic plate made by Wedgwood. £18

Cast iron spring balance scales with porcelain dial and base metal pan. £15

a tin plate version, to about £40 for one with a cast iron base and more if it has a brass dial. A marked Salter scale will cost about £50–£60 upwards.

The other domestic scales were made on a horizontal plane, with the weighing pan on one side, and an oblong platform on the other to take the weights (see: *Weights*). The base is usually cast iron (although a later model of the 1930s can have a weighted tinplate base), and the pans are made of base metal or brass. These were round, or in an oblong shape with rounded corners. A deep pan in a scoop shape with a wide lip was usually used commercially, but can still be an attractive addition to a collection. A brass pan is more collectable than one of base metal and the price reflects this, with examples starting at about £40. Scales with a base metal pan will cost about £25–£30.

A variation on this is the butter or dairy scale. Instead of a pan, these scales have a flat round or oblong ceramic plate. This was either white, or veined to resemble marble, and an Avery scale would have a plate made by Wedgwood veined with grey marbling. This will cost about £20 without weights.

SCALES, LETTER

As with the domestic scales (above) these postal scales fall into two types: the spring balance, and the type that worked on the see-saw principle and needed marked weights to balance the items weighed.

The spring balance scales were tiny, seldom more than 4 inches high. The dial was a curved oblong on the front of the base with a pointer that moved vertically up and down a central slot. They are reasonably priced at around £10–£12.

The other spring balance scale is the candlestick type about 6 or 7 inches tall and having a column base. These Victorian examples are dearer and one in brass will cost about £50 upwards.

Postal scales with weights made of brass were also brass, and were set on a polished wood base. The weights ranged from ½ to 8 ounces and were set in recesses cut into the wood. Prices for these are about £30. Check that no weights are missing, and that they match.

Scent Bottles — See Perfume Bottles, page 171

SCRIMSHAW

Most scrimshaw — the art of engraving or incising designs on certain bones — was done by sailors, especially whalers. The materials used were the ivory teeth of the sperm whale, whalebone, the tusks and bones of walruses and reindeer horns.

All kinds of small objects were made, such as paper knives, sewing tools and accessories, and medallions.

The bone was decorated with nautical scenes and pictures, or abstract designs. The more work there is on a whale's tooth, the more it will cost. A tusk showing Nelson's flagship *Victory* in fine detail, plus the figure of Britannia, the flag, and other figures, and dating from the mid-19th century will cost over £1000, but more modest pieces can be found for under £60.

The biggest danger for the collector is the reproduction and faking of scrimshaw. Old whale teeth, previously undecorated, are being inscribed, and the fake is difficult to detect. Modern reproductions are being made in plastic or polystyrene.

Brass mounted medallion with an engraving of a ship. £40

SEASIDE SOUVENIRS

Ribbon plate with gilded edge and transfer printed pattern. £25

Miniature Victorian purse showing the New Pier at Brighton. £22

The growth of railways in the 1840s made it easier for people to go on holiday, and resorts on or near a main line grew fast. The industry of commercially produced souvenirs for holidaymakers to take home with them also grew.

Transfer printing in the mid-1800s led to china and pottery souvenirs (see: *Blue and White Transfer Printed Ware*) and plates were made bearing scenes of resorts or views of local interest. Pink plates with a sepia or black and white scene are very collectable, as are ribbon plates. The latter had pierced borders in varying patterns, and ribbon was sometimes slotted through the holes. These plates were usually floral decorated. Both pink and ribbon plates will cost from £15 each.

Cups and saucers were produced, again in pink with a transfer printed view, or in white with a raised floral pattern and bearing a gilded message, such as, 'A Present from Skegness', or 'A Souvenir from Brighton'. These will cost about £12 for a cup and saucer. W.H. Goss made heraldic china for each town to show off its coat of arms (see: *Crested China*) and other factories quickly followed suit.

Shells were a natural souvenir and were used in a variety of ways — surrounding photograph frames, decorating dolls, even arranged to resemble complicated flower bouquets and placed under glass domes. Shells were also used for jewellery and delicate cameos were carved, necklaces of tiny shells made by the score. Jet jewellery from Whitby was another favourite (see: *Jet Jewellery*). Pebble jewellery from the Isle of Man, Cornwall and the east of

England consisted of polished beads of amber, agate, cornelian, jasper and bloodstone.

Sand from Alum Bay in the Isle of Wight was bottled in layers, providing a colourful memento, and these glass towers can be found reasonably priced at about £12–£15.

Wooden items from Tunbridge and the Scottish town of Mauchline were practical souvenirs (see: *Mauchline Ware* and *Tunbridgeware*). Holidaymakers could buy stamp boxes, napkin rings, sewing accessories and paper knives as mementoes of happy times.

Shaving Mugs — See Moustache Cups and Shaving Mugs, page 155

SHELLEY CHINA

F ormerly Foley China (Wileman & Co) the china was made by the Shelley Potteries from about 1925. The backstamp from 1925 to 1940 shows the name Shelley in script set within an elongated shield, with the word England beneath.

The factory produced extremely fine table china (see: *Cups and Saucers*). The

Art Deco cup and saucer from the 1930s with unusual hand-painted iris design. £25

Art Deco style of the late 1920s and 30s influenced designers. The tea cups have triangular handles, and were made in inverted conical shapes, decorated with bold abstract patterns. They were also made in curved octagonal shapes with stylized trees in black and yellow against a white ground. Orange, yellow, acid green and vivid blue were all used, and the motifs included sunbursts and peacock tails. A 6-place teaset in these styles will cost over £300, but it is possible to buy a cup and saucer from about £20.

The late 1930s and early 40s saw a return to the more traditional shapes and patterns. 'Woodland' features trees by a lake, the earth being carpeted with wild flowers in soft blue, pink and yellow. Bluebells, primroses and other wild flowers were used on other china, and the later pieces are cheaper, being about £12 for a cup and saucer.

SHOE HORNS

Travelling shoe kit comprising tortoiseshell horn and buttonhook. £18

These were made of horn, iron, brass, ivory, silver, steel and plastic, and there are many examples still to be found. The shoe horns were usually part of the accessories found in a travelling case, or were sold in boxed sets with button-hooks (see: *Buttonhooks*). Sometimes the two were combined into one item, the buttonhook swivelling neatly into the curve of the shoe horn.

As with buttonhooks, the interest of the shoe horn lies in the handle. Silver handled horns were elaborately chased, embossed or engraved. The hallmark was usually discreetly hidden in the pattern and can be hard to find. At the turn of the century, 'leg' handles became popular, but these will cost about £25 for the novelty value.

Travelling shoe horns were small, usually made of plastic (see: *Plastic*) and combined with a buttonhook, and sometimes a comb. They were intended for slipping in the pocket or handbag. Advertising horns are extremely interesting to collect. Messages such as 'Kiwi, the Quality Shoe Polish', 'Lotus Shoes, fitting in every sense', and 'Warners Footwear Ltd. Branches everywhere' would be stamped along the shoe horn. These will be about £15 upwards.

SHOES-CHINA & GLASS

The earliest examples of these are the blue and white clogs produced by the Delft factory in Holland, or in Bristol. Most shoes were made as souvenirs from the mid-19th century. The majority came from Germany which specialized in producing souvenirs for export (see: *Fairings*). Many are decorated with the name of the resort, or bear a photographic view of it. These were made in faintly lustred pink and will cost about £12–£15 each (see: *Seaside Souvenirs*). More ornate are the flower encrusted shoes in green or white. They were also gilded and sometimes have a message such as 'Love the Giver', or the name of the resort in gold writing. These cost about £15.

W. H. Goss and other manufacturers produced shoes and boots with heraldic crests (see: *Crested China*) and these will cost up to about £10. Clog-type shoes were made by the Dutch and the French firm of Quimper, and these rely on their bright colours for attractiveness. Bisque (unglazed porcelain) shoes were produced,

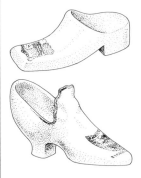

Top: A Goss crested shoe modelled on Queen Elizabeth's riding shoe. £70

Bottom: An Arcadian lady's shoe of Edwardian style. £8–£10

Pressed glass shoe made as a thimble holder in amber glass. £15

mainly by continental firms, and these have pastel flowers looking as if piped in icing.

Glass shoes are also very collectable and come in a variety of colours from clear glass through to dark blue, green, red and amber, even black. Some of the clear glass shoes were moulded to represent cut glass (see: *Press Moulded Glass*) and have steps on the insole intended to take glass cruets. Others were made as thimble holders, ink-wells, or salts.

Multi-coloured shoes were made of slag or marbled glass and can be found in green and white, or amethyst and white, and these will cost up to £25. Vaseline and cranberry examples will be dearer (see: *Cranberry Glass* and *Vaseline Glass*). If stamped with the maker's name, such as Sowerby, then plain coloured glass examples will be around £25–£30.

Reproductions are creeping on to the antique market, so check the shoe or boot carefully for any modern foreign backstamp.

SILVER SPOONS

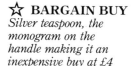

☆ **BARGAIN BUY**
Silver teaspoon, the monogram on the handle making it an inexpensive buy at £4

Plain undecorated silver teaspoons can cost as little as £5 each, so there is ample scope for the enthusiast to build up a representative collection. (see: *Caddy Spoons*). The smallest spoons are tiny salt

spoons about one inch long. They mostly have a shell shaped bowl which has been gilded as a protection against the corrosive action of the salt, and a thin handle ending in a gold knob. The price will be about £8. Plain examples with a more elongated bowl will be for mustard and will cost no more than £4 or £5 for a good hallmarked example.

The price of spoons depends on the weight of silver, the date of manufacture and the rarity of style, and the hallmark must be good and clear. For example, a Charles I apostle spoon dated 1639 will cost over £1000, whereas a silver christening spoon from the early 20th century will cost about £15–£20.

Early spoons had varying ends and finials and these can date a spoon approximately, *eg* Diamond Point (1500), Apostle (1600), Puritan (1650), Trefid (1680), Dog Nose (1700), Hanoverian (1720), Old English (1760), Fiddle (1820). But these shapes have been copied in later spoons as the hallmark will reveal. Other patterns on the handles were King's, Queen's and Thread and Shell.

Small spoons bearing the crests of towns were made as holiday souvenirs, and these are found from about £10. Teaspoons, once part of a set, can make interesting items to collect singly, and can be bought from about £5, depending on pattern and style. Spoons with ornate handles and finials will cost more.

Jam spoons with silver bowls, and handles made of silver, mother-of-pearl or bone will cost about £12–£15. Spoons of dessert size, with ornate embossing in the bowl, sometimes gilded, in a pattern of fruit and leaves are called berry spoons and will cost £15–£20.

Check the spoon for wear. Dessert spoons, for example, will have worn thin on one side; teaspoons will be thin at the tip and will have a tendency to curl.

19th-century berry spoon with embossed pattern. £60

SMALL SILVER

Many items were fashioned in silver in Victorian times, and small boxes make a good start to a collection. Card cases, vestas (match boxes) and needle holders were all made in silver. They could be square, round, oval or heart-shaped; embossed chased, engraved or machine turned. They will cost about £15 for a plain vesta case to about £40 for a card case. Snuff boxes in silver are rare, and prohibitively priced. Tiny vinaigrettes with their grills for a perfume soaked sponge (see: *Vinaigrettes*) sometimes had a ring attached and can be worn as a pendant. These cost from about £60. Watch chains or alberts can also be transformed into necklaces or bracelets and a heavy example will cost about £35. Check for the hallmark on the bar end, and that the snap attachment is original and silver.

Toilet articles, silver topped as part of a dressing table or travelling set, will consist of cylindrical bottles with cap shaped tops in embossed silver, and will cost from about £20. Double ended scent bottles in coloured glass, with silver tops (see: *Perfume Bottles*) will be about £40. Trinket items can be found with silver tops, such as powder bowls, oblong pin

Serviette ring, pepper pot and tooth powder box priced between £30 and £50

*Unusual egg cups.
£80 for the pair*

boxes with plain or engraved lids, and
hair tidies, which consisted of a bowl
shaped container with a circular silver top
having a large central hole. Check the
tops carefully as these are frequently
dented. Also check the inner rim of the
glass, which is prone to chipping. The
containers were plain, hand cut, or in
pressed glass, and will cost from £10 for
a pin box, to about £20–£25 for a good
powder bowl.

Silver handled scissors and tongs
make an interesting addition to a
collection. Asparagus tongs with their
wide perforated blades will be expensive,
but grape scissors with their vine and leaf
encrusted handles will be about £40–£50.
Sugar tongs can be plain, or ornately
engraved; ice tongs have bird's foot
claws. Napkin rings can be found for
under £10 if plain or inscribed with an
initial, more if heavily decorated. Fruit
knives (see: *Penknives and Fruit Knives*)
and butter knives will cost from £25,
depending on the amount of decoration
on the handle and/or blade, and cake
knives will be from £30. Silver salts are
expensive, but silver topped glass cruets
will be from about £10 each.

Silver handled items from manicure
sets, such as nail files, are still relatively
cheap at £5–£8, and the handles are plain,
or ornate. Buttonhooks and shoe horns
will cost from £15, depending on size,
although tiny glove hooks will be dearer.

*Small heart-shaped
Victorian frame with
attractive embossing.
£50*

Chain purses made of silver mesh will cost £30 upwards, again depending on size. Larger examples can cost £60. Check that the chain linking is intact with no holes. Silver thimbles are very collectable and these start from about £15. Early examples are dearer, and check that the hallmark is clear. Sterling silver is always cheaper than hallmarked silver.

Silver photograph frames start at about £20–£25 for one about 3 by 4 inches and ornately embossed, up to about £90 for a large studio size. Modern imitations are being made so check the date of the hallmark. Bradbury's Book of Hallmarks is a must for the silver collector, and is usefully pocket sized.

Brooches can be found for under £10, with name brooches being about £15 (see: *Name Brooches*). A silver chain necklace in belcher style, approximately 27 inches long will cost £30–£35; a chain bracelet with heart shaped padlock will be about £20.

Tiny silver shoes, animals, egg-shaped nutmeg graters, and babies' rattles are all collectable and will cost from about £20.

SNUFF BOXES

These can be distinguished from any other small box by the unique hinge, whereby the lid and base dovetail into each other so neatly and closely that an airtight seal is formed. Silver snuff boxes are so expensive and rare, they are out of reach of the ordinary collector, but several other examples can be found.

Snuff boxes were made in wood decorated with transfer printed pictures or mosaic veneering (see: *Mauchline Ware* and *Tunbridgeware*) and these will cost from about £25–£30. A horn example will

Snuff box (approximately 3 inches in length) inlaid with mother-of-pearl in a chequer board design. £30

be about £40–£60 in good condition.

Papier mâché was used extensively and a small oblong snuff box in plain black will cost about £15. The boxes were sometimes painted with classical scenes or floral patterns, and prices start at £25–£30. Check the hinge, for usage will weaken it.

Metal boxes were made in gunmetal, or plated, and new manufacturing techniques in the mid-1800s enabled boxes to be made in octagonal shapes. If the plating is worn the box is devalued, but in good condition will cost about £20. Any enamelling will add value and a fine example will cost over £60.

SPELTER FIGURES

Originally made to simulate bronze, lead and ormolu, spelter is an alloy in which zinc is the principal constituent. This makes it light and prone to damage, so check any piece carefully before buying.

The most prolific period of manufacture was between the 1870s and 1890s when figures, both classical and allegorical, were made in quantity, although manufacture did continue up

Bronzed spelter figure circa 1910. £45

until the 1920s. In order to get the 'bronze' look, the silvery white metal was artificially bronzed and this can be detected by scratching the base of the article where it will not be seen.

Some castings were better than others, and in cheap spelter figures, the definition is poor, the figures very lightweight. But a good heavy figure can be well worth having. Some pieces are signed and dated on the back of the base, and will sometimes also have the factory stamp. Look out for this, as it will add value to the piece.

Pairs of figures were popular, such as the French 'La Paix' and 'Le Travail' — male and female fisher folk who stood about 12 to 14 inches high. This pair will cost about £80. French spelter figures representing the seasons can also be found but often these are of inferior quality and will cost £30 each. If the quality is good the price will be nearer £45–£55 each.

Horses modelled in spelter were popular and a rearing 'Marley' horse with unmounted rider standing beside it will cost about £70. Check that the reins are intact. Military figures suffer the loss of spears, so again check carefully.

Art Nouveau and Art Deco figures were frequently copied from the bronze. Art Nouveau examples will cost from about £80 for a 12-inch model of a girl with flowing hair and draperies. Fairies and cherubs will cost more. But Art Deco figures about 6 to 8 inches high, set on an onyx plinth, will cost from about £30. These are frequently painted or gilded and show girls in stylized dancing poses. If painted, check for chipping or flaking, and check the base for cracks or chips.

Spoons — See Caddy Spoons, page 41, Love Spoons, page 142, Silver Spoons, page 206, Sugar Sifter Spoons, page 219.

STAFFORDSHIRE DOGS

The majority of these were made between 1830 and 1910 and they were modelled mainly as greyhounds, poodles or spaniels, although other breeds were also produced. Sizes vary between 5 and 18 inches. Some were intended as mantel dogs.

Greyhounds were usually small, the largest about 10 inches in height, and an example of one of these (or a whippet) standing on an oval base dating from about 1850 will cost about £40–£60. (A matching pair will cost over £200.) Dalmatian style dogs were also made, and a late example of 1860 will be about £90.

Poodles were made with the Dutch or lion-style clip to their fur. This leaves the hair around the shoulders long, with the hindquarters sheared. A small pair of cream-coloured poodles 4½ inches tall will cost about £70. The poodles can have roughened fur and wear a perky expression, or be less well modelled with smoother fur and a doleful expression.

The Staffordshire spaniel is the dog most frequently found at antique fairs. These were made in white, black and white, or red (orange) and white. They frequently have gilded chains attached to a padlock on a collar around their necks, and wear a rather surprised expression. Good dogs, which are usually earlier, have well defined fur, well marked whiskers and eyes. Later examples are less well made and sometimes had glass eyes fixed into the cavities. All mantel dogs were left- or right-facing. A pair of well made spaniels in black and white with gilt collars will cost about £70; a single dog about £30. Larger dogs are more expensive. Look out for a realistic King

Victorian spaniel with chain and padlock on the collar. £50

A rather worn dog with indistinct features in black and white. £25

Charles spaniel — an example of this about 8 or 9 inches high could be worth almost £200.

STAFFORDSHIRE FIGURES & FLATBACKS

Spill holder of the 1850s, the colours vivid. These spill holders are not rare and will cost between £25 and £40

Although Staffordshire figures made their appearance about 1740, the majority of collectable ones to be found today are Victorian and date from about 1840. Made as chimney ornaments, the figures depict life, events and personalities of the day (see: *Staffordshire Portrait Figures*).

Early figures stood on flat oval bases and were decorated in vivid colours of orange, green and cobalt blue. They are more well defined in the modelling than the later 'flat back' figures. Towards the 1860s, the colours were toned down and more gilt was applied.

Figures can be grouped under royal, political, military and religious headings. In the miscellaneous section one can place rustic scenes such as 'Cottage Girl', 'Village Group', or 'The Blacksmith', and these will cost between £100 and £300.

Unnamed figures are considerably less. A figure group dated about 1850 with a man and woman standing beside a tree with a hollow trunk will cost about £70; a brightly coloured huntsman, his cloak draped casually over his shoulders will be about £80 — mounted and dated at about 1890, he will be only £30–£40. A pair of fruit sellers (man and wife) holding their baskets of fruit, also about 1850 will cost just over £100.

It is worth shopping around at an antique fair as prices vary considerably.

Beware of imitations and reproductions, although these are usually quite easily recognizable by their lack of definition and spontaneity.

Restored and damaged figures are considerably cheaper, and if the damage is confined to a minor crack, might well be acceptable. Crazing will appear on older pieces; this can be imitated on reproductions but is usually so regular as to be noticeable.

STAFFORDSHIRE PORTRAIT FIGURES

Portrait figures can be divided into various groups: royal, political, religious and military (see: *Staffordshire Figures and Flatbacks*). There are believed to be seventeen different models of Queen Victoria depicted sitting, standing, riding, crowned, and reading a book, and about sixteen figures of Prince Albert in various poses. Some other members of the Victorian royal family also featured, including the Prince of Wales, Princess Royal, and Princess Alexandra (later Queen Alexandra). Some of the royal figures cost almost £300, but one can find a portrait of the Prince of Wales shown standing beside his dog for about £90. It lacks the variety and depth of colour used on different examples, but they cost twice the amount. Figures of the Princess Royal (mounted) cost about £70, dated about 1850, and a figure of Charles I on horseback costs about £40, dated about 1910. Other monarchs include King John, Henry V, Henry VIII and William III.

Politicians include Disraeli, Cobden, Gladstone and Parnell. The Duke of Wellington was a favourite and about fourteen figures of him were made. These

BARGAIN BUY
This miniature figure of Napoleon (some damage to the back) was bought for only £15

range between 6½ inches to 18 inches high, and the prices range accordingly, between £90 and £800. Robert Peel figures cost between £250 for a portrait bust to about £4,000 for a rare equestrian pose 13½ inches high.

Military portrait figures cover such varied subjects as the 'Death of Nelson', Napoleon, equestrian figures of Lord Raglan, Sir George Brown, Omar Pasha, and so on. Prices range from about £100 for a figure group 'The Soldier's Return' 8¾ inches high, and progress upwards for known military figures.

Other groups include theatre, opera, ballet, circus, crime, sport, authors and fictional characters, poets and composers. Prices start at about £75 for a figure of young Lochinvar bearing away the maiden on horseback.

STATIONERY BOXES

Small compartmented box in papier mâché, from the mid-19th century. £60

Some examples of these can cost no more than £15 or £20 and were made in oak or mahogany. They consisted of a slanting box without a lid, the sections being divided by lengths of wood slotted into compartments. They were intended to hold paper, envelopes, visiting cards etc, and are the most simple kind of stationery box.

More elaborate examples were made in mahogany, oak, rosewood, coramandel and walnut. These were made in three parts: the main body of the box having sections for stationery and papers, the front flap dropping down to reveal a blotter, the top hinging upwards to show the inkwells, pen tray and, sometimes, a set of letter scales (see: *Scales — Letter*). These boxes will cost considerably more at about £250, although less elaborate versions can be found for about £150.

Another, cabinet type, is an upright box with a sloping front and two opening doors. They reveal a slotted section for notes, paper, envelopes, etc, inkwells and a pen tray. The interior surface of the doors have criss-cross ribbon or webbing which would be used for the insertion of visiting cards, notes, reminders etc. These stationery boxes are more reasonably priced at about £60–£80. Check the key is available and working, and that the doors are in sound condition and not warped in any way.

Some cabinets have shelved interiors with a roll top front, and these will cost about £100. It is important to determine that the roll top functions smoothly without sticking.

STRAINERS & DRAINERS

The flat ceramic oval 'plates' pierced with holes were made to fit into a shallow dish. The meat or fish was then placed on the strainer and the excess water or meat juices would drain through. They vary in size, but about 10–12 inches across the widest part is most usual. Round strainers can occasionally be found but these are rare, and will cost over £100.

The drain holes were arranged in patterns, groups of small circular holes, or sometimes in more elaborately pierced groups. This patterning is more apparent when the strainer is viewed from behind. The decorative patterns were in blue and white (see: *Blue and White Transfer Printed Ware*), and these are of enormous variety.

Some patterns were simple groups of flowers with a central single bud, others

An attractively decorated strainer, patterned with flowers in a strong blue. £40

S

were more elaborate, such as a view of a ruined castle or abbey set in parkland against a background of trees, or perhaps with a large urn in the foreground set beside a lake, with two men in the Chinese sailing vessel, and a pagoda in the background.

Colours vary between a rich deep cobalt blue, or a pale clear blue, through to an almost greenish tone. Some can be found in brown or even plain white with no pattern at all, but these are less collectable.

The strainers were rarely marked on the reverse with a backstamp, so attribution can be difficult. Sometimes the holes give a clue but recognizing the printed pattern is a more sure way. Prices range between £20 for a simply decorated example to about £60 for a late Victorian piece with good scenic content.

SUGAR CASTERS

They first made their appearance during the reign of Charles II and have been in constant use ever since. Originally silver, casters were then made in silver plate, glass, china and pottery.

The shapes vary from a straight-sided cylindrical caster to a convoluted baluster shape. The tops are invariably silver plated and can be pierced with holes in groups, or patterned with the holes in curves, clover leaf-shapes or crosses. The caps either push on or are threaded to be screwed on.

Glass Victorian sugar casters were made in clear glass, and were hand cut or sharply moulded (see: *Press Moulded Glass*) or in coloured glass, usually dark green or cranberry (see: *Cranberry Glass*). The latter are usually panelled and straight sided. A cranberry caster will cost about £25 upwards, a press moulded

Four casters including Royal Winton (left) and cranberry glass (front) ranging in price between £12 and £40

218

example about £15. Check that the cap will ease off, or that it is not cross-threaded and impossible to remove. Also check the plating for wear.

China casters can have plated tops or, if dating from the 1930s, be filled from the bottom, the hole being plugged with a cork. The greatest variety of shapes occur in china and pottery and the price range varies accordingly, from about £8 for a simple example with little decoration to about £30–£40 for an Art Deco piece by Clarice Cliff (see: *Cliff, Clarice*).

SUGAR SIFTER SPOONS

These can have a patterned or plain bowl and were made in silver and silver plate. Larger than a teaspoon, almost dessert spoon size, the spoons have an elaborate pattern of piercing on the bowl to allow the sugar to fall freely. Sometimes the bowl was patterned with fruit and foliage similar to berry spoons (see: *Small Silver*) with the handle ornately chased or engraved. The spoons will cost about £10 upwards in silver plate, more in silver.

The teaspoon size with a bowl patterned in round or shaped holes, and having a pointed end, was used for skimming the tea leaves that floated to the surface. The point of the spoon was a handy implement to free the clogged spout of the teapot also. These are more unusual and will cost over £30 if silver.

Silver-plated sifter spoon with shell-shaped bowl. £12

SYLVAC POTTERY

M ade by Shaw and Copestake, Sylvac pottery dates from about 1936. The first backstamp shows a flower-like circle containing the words Sylvac Semi-Porcelain. Made in England. From 1946, the backstamp shows Sylvac Ware. Made in England, written in script. Sometimes Sylvac was impressed in capital letters underneath the glaze, but this can sometimes be blurred and difficult to interpret.

The ware most popularly collected has a semi-matt glaze and portrays animals such as rabbits, dogs, and occasionally cats, in green, beige, blue — and more rarely — a bright acid yellow. Elves nestling against tree trunks to form flower holders can also be found. Prices are still relatively modest. A small dog 3 or 4 inches high will cost £5 or £6; a larger dog about 12–14 inches high will be about £20. The cats are more stylized than the dogs, and have their tails standing on end as if surprised. The rabbits, too are less lifelike, and have rounded, storybook shapes. Prices for both these vary between £4 and £7 for a small example.

Small Sylvac dog in green matt glaze. £6

Sylvac ventured in Art Deco stylized ware too, and large plaques can be found in beige and pastel shades decorated with stylized trees in soft, muted colours. These are about £40–£60. Vases and small dishes are £15–£20.

Shaw and Copestake also made pottery before the Sylvac mark was introduced, and the backstamp shows a flower-shaped circle containing a petalled flower inside and the words Made in England. This mark dates the item from 1925 to 1936, and a clock with garnitures (see: *China Cased Clocks*) will cost about £40–£50 for the set.

TAPE MEASURES

Tape measures were not marked in inches until the mid-1800s; previously they had been marked in nails, a measurement of 2¼ inches. Early tape ribbons were made of silk but many have rotted and care must be taken when extending them from their cases.

Victorian measures were made in wood, ivory or bone, mother-of-pearl, metal, and later, of synthetic materials (see: *Bakelite* and *Plastic*). They were operated by a wind-on handle, but later a spring mechanism was used.

The tape measures made in wood and ivory were round, pierced or carved, in the shape of a crown or barrel, or cotton reel shaped. Wooden examples were decorated with transfer printing, or a mosaic veneer (see: *Mauchline Ware* and *Tunbridgeware*).

Metal measures had an infinite variety of shapes: water mills, coffee grinders, kettles, shoes, clocks, animals and birds. They could be round pill-box shapes with a tiny animal or cherub perched on the lid, or have scenes of popular resorts or views (see: *Seaside Souvenirs*).

Plastic tape measures were shaped like ships, shells, mirrors, flat irons, baskets of fruit and flowers, dice, and hats.

Rare tape measure in the shape of a bird cage, 3 inches high. £50

Ivory (left) and wooden tape measures from the late 19th century. £15–£30

Prices vary, but will start at about £10 for a simple example in wood or plastic, more if silver or early. Novelty items will be about £20. Check that the spring mechanism works, and that the tape is not too rotten, although sometimes renewal was inevitable and can be acceptable.

TEAPOTS

Sadler's 'Ye Dainty Ladyee' teapot in pale green. £15

Tea has been drunk since the late 1600s and the teapot dates from this time. Teapots have always been decorative as well as functional, and pottery and china examples followed the shapes of silver teapots at first, although a Staffordshire stoneware teapot was made in the shape of a house as early as about 1750. Cauliflower shapes also appeared at this time as did pineapples, cabbages, a camel, and a seated mandarin. Later teapots were round and pot-bellied, or straight-sided with oval or round bodies, and it was not until the late 19th century that the novelty teapot made its appearance again, when the Aesthetic teapot showed the top half of an effeminate dandy.

The Victorian teapot is very collectable and turn of the century examples can be found for no more than £15–£20. One of the most prolific makers was the firm of James Sadler who began production in 1899. His earthenware teapots were stamped J.S.S.B. until 1937 when the name Sadler, Burslem appeared. Other manufacturers to look out for are Gibson, Worcester, Davenport, Minton, Spode, Coalport, Wedgwood and Belleek. Victorian examples of their teapots will cost about £40–£60 upwards, depending on the manufacturer, and whether made of china or pottery.

Unmarked earthenware teapots are

cheaper, and there is no lack of variety, shape or design. They can be found with floral decorations against a cream background, in dark blue and orange and heavily gilded, and these will cost about £20–£25. Check that the spout is not chipped, and that the handle is firmly fixed and has not been re-glued.

Twentieth century teapots are also collectable, especially those of the 1930s. Art Deco teapots were made, such as the geometric shapes by Clarice Cliff (see: *Cliff, Clarice*), and Shelley (see: *Shelley China*). Teapots by Sadler include ones shaped like racing cars, the driver's head being the knob on the lid, and a long-skirted lady. Lingard made a teapot resembling Charles Dickens' character, Mr Pickwick, and Price Brothers and Grimwades made them shaped like cottages and houses (see: *Cottage Ware*). These cost about £15–£20 for Sadler's lady, to £30 for a cottage-style teapot.

Unmarked Victorian teapot of attractive rococo design. £40

THIMBLES & CASES

A s with most sewing accessories, thimbles were made in various materials: silver, brass, steel sandwiched between two layers of silver, aluminium, base metal and plastic.

Silver thimbles were ornately decorated around the base, with flowers and leaves, the fleur-de-lis, commemorative patterns, messages and pictures, and inscriptions, and these will cost from about £20. Silver-encased steel thimbles were mostly made by Dorcas, Dreema and Dura. They were usually plain, with the name of the maker stamped along the edge, but sometimes were made more attractive by surrounding the indentations with flower-like motifs.

Collectable silver thimble made by Charles Horner. £60

Unusual bone thimble case with star-shaped decoration. £50

Aluminium thimbles often carried advertising messages on a coloured band near the rim. All manner of wares were advertised: Nestle's Milk, Cerebos Salt, Crawfords Biscuits, Lyon's Cakes, Nugget Boot Polish, and the *News of the World* newspaper. Plain aluminium thimbles will cost £2 or £3, but those carrying advertising slogans will be about £8–£10.

Good quality thimbles were kept in cases and these were made of wood, mother-of-pearl, tortoiseshell, silver, plate and brass, and were lined with velvet in rose pink, green, or dark blue. They were made to resemble miniature knife boxes, shoes, trunks, or binoculars, the latter holding a pair of thimbles. They were round, oval, octagonal, or egg-shaped.

Wooden cases were made with transfer printed designs, and decorated with mosaic veneer (see: *Mauchline Ware* and *Tunbridgeware*), or could be replica acorns which unscrewed to reveal the thimble. Tiny high-heeled shoes were made in glass, silver, or covered with brocade or velvet. Other novelties included top hats, pipes, bulldogs, baskets, barrels and buckets, some being bead-covered (see: *Beadwork*).

Prices vary between £15–£20 for a tartan covered egg, to £25 upwards for a silver horseshoe-shaped holder.

TILES

Tiles have been with us since medieval times when churches used them on their floors, but it was not until the 17th century that the idea caught on again when Delft tiles were used in the home, on the walls, as skirtings, and in fireplaces. An English Delft tile made in Bristol or Lambeth around 1750 will cost

between £25 and £60 depending on clarity
of pattern.

The firm of Minton began making tiles
in 1793 but it was not until the mid-1800s
that production became successful, and by
the 20th century was firmly established.
Other early manufacturers were Copeland
and Garrett, Chamberlain's of Worcester,
and later, Maw and Co, W. Godwin,
T & R Boote, Malkin Edge, Pilkington's,
Wedgwood and Doulton.

Tiles were used on walls, fireplaces, as
splash backs for washstands, and
umbrella stands. Designs in the late 19th
century were influenced by the Arts and
Crafts Movement. Art Nouveau designs
inspired the makers and tiles were made
in flowing patterns both in transfer
printing and in relief. Tube-lining was
also a popular form of decoration (see:
Rhead, Charlotte) in the 1900s, and flower
patterns appeared in rich and vivid
colours. Tube-lined tiles (unmarked with
maker's name) will cost between £15 and
£30 each depending on the design.
Unmarked but colourful Victorian tiles
will cost from about £5.

Some tiles were made in sets or panels
and these are extremely collectable. They
can fetch hundreds of pounds, especially
if identifiable as designed by William De
Morgan, or made by Minton or Doulton.
A set depicting the story of Cinderella and
designed by Burne-Jones was recently
sold in a London auction room for no less
than £11,000.

*Dutch Delft tile in blue
and white. £15*

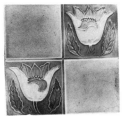

*Left: Art Nouveau
tile showing sleeping
beauty, £25, and (right)
a quartered Victorian
tile in green and pink.
£6*

T

TINS

Round, square, oval, octagonal — these are only a few of the shapes in which novelty tins were made. Tins were manufactured to resemble a brass bound trunk, in the shapes of houses, shops and castles, or painted in imitation of Wedgwood's Jasper ware in blue and white. They originally contained tea, biscuits, sweets or toffees, for example, or the product that was advertised on the lid, such as Oxo cubes, Coleman's mustard, Quorn custard powder, or a brand of tooth powder. Prices begin at £2 or £3 for an Oxo cube tin four inches square.

Advertising tins were also made to commemorate royal occasions, and a Cadbury's chocolate tin made for the silver jubilee of George V and Queen Mary will cost about £12. Other tins featuring royalty were those made to send out to the troops during the Boer War and the First World War. The Boer War tin, which was packed with chocolate, was designed by Barclay & Fry of Southwark, and they printed the design straight on to the metal. It bore a gold embossed

A selection of gramophone needle tins, about £3–£5 each

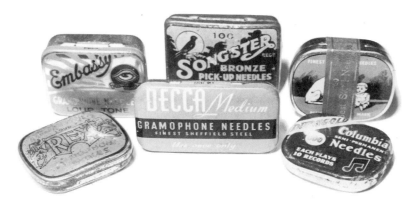

medallion of Queen Victoria set against a red background. The queen's cypher was on one side of the portrait, the words 'South Africa 1900' on the other. A facsimile handwritten message from the queen ran along the lid. The Princess Mary tin was made in 1914 and was of embossed brass. The box contained tobacco, a pipe, lighter, a photograph of Princess Mary, and a Christmas card. It sells today for about £8–£10 minus its contents.

Cigarette tins include brands such as Gold Flake, Gold Leaf, Navy Cut, and Murray's Mellow Smoking Mixture, and prices for these are between £3 and £14.

Gramophone needle tins are also collectable and still reasonably cheap at £2 to £3 upwards. Columbia and Edison Bell are among the names on the tins.

It is important that the paintwork on the tin is in reasonably good condition, and that the tin itself is not too battered and dented. Check that the hinges are in good shape too, as often the wires that held the interlocking parts together become damaged and snap off.

TOAST RACKS

Toast racks made in silver, plate, pewter, china and pottery come in varying shapes and sizes. The smallest example was intended for the bachelor's, or one-person, breakfast tray.

The divisions between the slices of toast can vary. Some resemble slices of bread, others have a heraldic look with a knight holding crossed spears, embellished with gilding, and the latter will cost about £10. Victorian china toast racks, decorated with transfer printing, will cost between £10 and £15, though for a good blue and white example one can add on at least another £5 (see: *Blue and White Transfer Printed Ware*).

Toast racks were made which incorporated marmalade and jam dishes. These can either have a shallow dish at each end, or a square lidded pot in the middle. Egg cups come with toast racks, too, and one example with the divisions looking as if made of gilded rope has a floral egg cup at each end. These cost from about £15.

In the 1930s toast racks became part of the Art Deco scene, as did all tableware, and they were decorated in vivid colours and patterns. Carlton made them with flowers in relief; Shelley painted them in drip-like patterns of green, orange and yellow, and Grimwades

Unmarked ceramic toast rack made in the 1930s, the jam and butter sections decorated with flowers. £12

placed roses on them, or decorated them with elves. These examples cost about £15 upwards.

Silver toast racks cost over £100, and novelty ones in plate will be well over £50. More ordinary racks in good condition will cost about £10 for a two-slice rack, about £25 for a larger one. Pewter toast racks cost from £9–£10.

TOBACCO JARS

M ade in earthenware or heavy pottery, the most collectable of tobacco jars are those made by Doulton. These are round lidded pots in stoneware, the better quality ones having the lid held on by a three-armed clip with a brass screw, ensuring air-tightness. Colours are dark: blue, brown or green, sometimes beige with figures of dogs and huntsmen in cream. Prices vary between £25 and £40 upwards. Ensure that the lid is not chipped and that it fits tightly. Other tobacco jars follow the same shape and general design and these are less expensive.

Some tobacco jars, particularly those made by Doulton, had a space in the knob of the lid to hold a sponge. These jars were usually made to hold ¼ lb, ½ lb, and 1 lb of tobacco. Jars made in Staffordshire pottery usually had a more delicate floral surface design.

Tobacco jars were also made in metal, and a cylindrical brass jar with close fitting lid will cost about £15–£30. A square cast iron Victorian box-type with a figure of Napoleon as the finial will cost about £35–£45, and an example in lead with a negro's head will be about £35–£40. Pewter jars of the Victorian period, simple in design, are about £45 and £55.

Small pottery tobacco jar in beige with attractive and appropriate lid. £18

Late Victorian tobacco jar depicting Mr Punch and his dog Toby. £55

TOBY JUGS

The traditional toby jug shows the seated figure of a man, a tricorn hat on his head, a jug of ale in his hand, a tankard or a churchwarden pipe in the other.

The origins of the toby are vague, some think it is based on Sir Toby Belch in Shakespeare's *Twelfth Night*, others contest the jug is based on the genial Uncle Toby in *Tristram Shandy*, while Toby Philpott, a character mentioned in the old song 'Little Brown Jug' is a third contender.

Royal Doulton have continued the tradition of the jugs since their first production in 1939. Falstaff, one of the early jugs, is still in production today — sure proof of its popularity. Double XX or The Man on the Barrel was withdrawn in 1969, and The Best is Not Too Good was withdrawn in 1940. Other jugs include Happy John, Honest Measure, and the Huntsman. Doulton toby jugs start at about £30 depending on size and whether or not it is still in production, but their version of a jug for Charrington's will cost about £150–£180.

Other makers such as Shorter and Wilkinson's also made jugs, as did the Devon potteries, and a Shorter jug will start at about £20.

A typical Toby jug of the early 20th century. £60

TOOLS

The most popular item in this section is the woodworking plane, especially the bench plane such as a jointer, smoother and jack plane made in beechwood. Of these, the 8-inch smoothing plane is most commonly found and will cost about £12 if in fine condition. The jack plane is more expensive at about £16–£20, but these are prices for early 20th-century examples — a beechwood draw plane of 1815 will cost almost £200, while a 19th-century cooper's plane will be about £70.

Special purpose planes such as routers, bead and rabbet planes are also collectable and can be found in good condition for between £20–£40. A beech and brass plough plane will cost £25–£30. Check that the blades are bright and entire. Rust often attacks the blades, and wear will reduce their length to unusable proportions.

Chisels of all types were used for woodwork and those made between 1880 and 1930 are collectable. A 30-inch chisel with a brass collar will cost about £50, although cheaper ones can be found.

Spirit levels are sought after, and a fine mahogany and brass example some 10 inches long will cost about £40, a simpler elm and brass level will be about £12, and a brass level 12 inches long is about £20.

Other collectable tools include boxwood rulers (£5–£20), ebony and brass mortice gauges (£10–£15), claw hammers (about £5), glass cutters (from £4), hacksaws (about £10–£15), and beechwood braces (between £50 and £100).

A beechwood brace with brass mountings. £60

TORQUAY & DEVON POTTERY

Most people associate the Devon potteries with motto ware and indeed much was made there, but the potteries also produced very fine work that can be loosely termed art pottery. The main factories were the Torquay Terracotta Company at Hele Cross, Aller

Two vases showing the stylized leaf designs. The larger vase would cost about £20–£25, the smaller, but more unusual about £22

Vale Pottery, Watcombe Pottery and the Longpark Pottery Company. Other potteries in the area were Tor Vale Art Pottery, Daison Pottery, Barton Pottery, Hart and Moist (Exeter Art Pottery), Devon Tors, and Bovey Tracey Pottery.

Terracotta plaques were made at Watcombe, the harsh red of the clay being toned down by the addition of white clay from Newton Abbot, and a large plaque, 24 inches across with a pattern of flowers and leaves was recently purchased for £20 — a rare bargain. Terracotta busts were made at both Watcombe and Torquay as were vases, and a small vase with some glazing, 5 or 6 inches high can be bought for under £100.

Decoration on the wares included *sgraffito* (where the design is 'scratched' into the glaze, showing the red clay beneath), the use of enamels, and engine turning. A footed shallow bowl has a pattern of ribbing with enamelled beading above and on the rim and foot. A double gourd-shaped vase would have engine turned parallel ridges and mask-head handles. An example of *sgraffito* work was used on a goblet-shaped vase with a pattern of trailing leaves and flowers cut into the slip, the whole then having an amber glaze. A gourd-shaped vase was made by Watcombe Pottery with a *sgraffito* picture of rams on the moors.

Lidded jars were made, with underglaze colours running into each other, and a beaker shows a pattern of stylized stencil-like flowers. Three handled vases of baluster shape, jugs with pinched and folded rims, puzzle jugs, toby jugs, and face jugs were all produced, and a face jug will cost £50 or £60.

Early wares were unmarked, and as a vast amount of Devon pottery was produced, the enthusiast would do well to get in touch with the Torquay Pottery Collector's Society.

T

TREEN

The word treen covers all small collectable items made in wood, including objects as varied as cups made from coconut shells, small boxes, cotton reel stands, nutmeg graters, egg timers and candlesticks. Mauchline and Tunbridgeware are also included (see: *Mauchline Ware* and *Tunbridgeware*).

Almost anything is grist to the treen collector's mill, and the price range is so wide that everyone can afford something. A string holder for example, can be as little as £8 or £12 for a late Victorian example, to £150 for one shaped like an acorn, and made of lignum vitae (a black wood from the West Indies), dated 1775.

Curiosities such as a vet's fleam hammer will be £25, an auctioneer's gavel will cost between £5 for a beech one, to £25 for a Georgian boxwood example. A Victorian darning aid with an egg-shaped knob at each end, made in boxwood will cost £5–£8.

Goblets were made in oak, sycamore, mahogany or walnut and can cost over £100. A cup made from a coconut shell mounted in silver will be over £400,

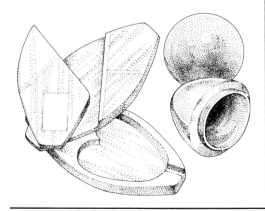

Left: A 'puzzle' snuff box in mahogany. £35–£40 as it is so unusual

Right: A thimble holder in sycamore. £20

whereas one made a hundred years later in 1800 and embellished with pewter will be only £30 or £40. Egg cups bought singly will cost £2 or £3 each, but a set of 10 on a stand, made in laburnum and mahogany will be nearer £500.

TRINKET SETS

These were made in glass, china and pottery, and ebony, and were intended for use on a dressing table.

An ebony set consisted of a tray, candlesticks, various lidded pots, a ring stand, sometimes a watch stand (see: *Watch Stands*) and hatpin holder. Sometimes the sets would be plain, or embellished with a silver initial.

Glass and porcelain sets would also consist of a tray, a pair of candlesticks, ring holder and trinket pots (lidded). There could also be a hatpin holder which could look like a large pepper shaker or a candlestick without a rim (see: *Hatpins and Holders*), a hair tidy, a pin box or tray, and occasionally matching scent bottles (see: *Perfume Bottles*). Glass sets were popular in moulded glass (see: *Press Moulded Glass*) in late Victorian times and these would either have matching lids and stoppers, or ones in silver. A glass set of the late Victorian era will cost about £40.

Colours from the 1920s onwards were pale green, pink, blue or amber. Or the sets could be made in cloud glass — an opaque glass with threads of colour rather like cigarette smoke. These were coloured amber, amethyst or blue, and a complete set with candlesticks, two trinket pots and ring stand on matching tray will be about £50.

China sets were variously decorated. A Japanese Noritaké set hand-painted in a soft blue and mauve, depicting a scene by a lake will cost about £75.

Art Deco trinket set in amber glass, a small chip to the tray. £40

T

TUNBRIDGEWARE

Prices for Tunbridgeware vary
enormously depending on the size and
condition of the object, and the
complexity of the design. But the beauty
of Tunbridgeware for the collector is that
it was produced in so much variety, that
there is something for everyone. Small
boxes can be found for as little as £20,
and offer a good opportunity for the
beginner to start a collection of these
beautifully veneered items, with their
mosaic surfaces featuring bold geometric
patterns or delicate floral sprays.

It wasn't until the early 1800s that
Tunbridgeware was made in its now
familiar form. The basic method used to
create the mosaic patterns entailed taking
strips of veneer, about six inches long by
one sixteenth thick, and placing them in
blocks corresponding to a pattern worked
out previously on graph paper — similar
to the technique employed by
glassmakers when arranging canes of
glass rods to form the intricate patterns of
paperweights. Once the block had been
built up to form the design, a thin layer
was sawn off the end (like cutting a slice
off a loaf). The resultant mosaic veneer

*Selection of
Tunbridgeware
including a matchbox,
watch stand, kettle
holder, small pin box,
and a stickware
necklace. Prices between
£25 and £60, although
the beads, being rare,
will cost almost £300*

235

T

Small decorative pillbox in a geometric design. £25

Attractive candle holder in polished wood. £35

was then glued on to the object that required decorating and carefully polished.

By this method, patterns of great complexity could be composed readily, comprised of many hundreds of tiny pieces of veneer. Stickware was another variation, using larger pieces of wood for bolder and more geometric designs.

The subtlety of the patterns relied on the selection of variously coloured woods which were employed in numerous combinations; altogether some 160 different types were used. Originally, no wood was dyed, and the rarest and most sought-after colour was green. This shade developed naturally when local tree species were attacked by fungus. These diseased trees were in short supply and, after about 1860, satinwood was stained a similar colour. Early 19th-century examples adorned with green mosaic designs are in demand today, and achieve high prices.

A bewildering number of Tunbridgeware items were produced, but all were useful and functional. Small articles designed to appeal to ladies included sewing accessories, book markers, pin trays, watch stands, glove boxes, pill boxes, button boxes — indeed, boxes of every size and for every purpose. Tea caddies were popular, sometimes with one compartment, or divided into two for the blending of tea. Cigarette, jewellery and writing boxes were also made, and desk accessories in the form of pen trays, stamp boxes, paper knives, inkstands and writing sets are found with a rich array of decorative designs. In addition, yo-yos and toys were made.

Small pieces of furniture were adorned with intricate mosaic patterns, and side tables, cigar tables, occasional and work tables can all be found for those who have several hundred pounds to spend.

VASELINE GLASS

Although many different types of yellow and green glass were produced throughout Europe in the 19th century, vaseline glass is distinctive for its oily, yellowish-green colour — similar in shade to the vaseline jelly or ointment bought in chemist's shops. This special colour was created by the use of uranium, and through processes of re-heating it varied in intensity from an opalescent cream to a bright transparent yellow. In some English examples the yellow may appear thick and opaque, while in Bohemia richer opalescent yellows and acid greens were developed of more intense hues.

Victorian posy holder in twisted pattern of Vaseline glass. £35

A number of vaseline items were produced in Europe and America from c.1835–1900, but perhaps most bizarre were the strangely twisted table decorations·so beloved by the Victorians. The centres of dining tables were adorned frequently with arrangements of glass ornaments, featuring tubelike vases with protuberances resembling the trunks of trees, complete with twig-like nodules. Such examples are hard to find in perfect condition due to their numerous fragile parts and branches. Some pieces were produced in cranberry glass, although vaseline table ornaments appear more commonly. Press-moulded candlesticks and small decorative baskets were also manufactured.

Fairy nightlamps and lampshades of vaseline colour provide a warm, sympathetic glow, while pieces displayed on a window sill will give a stunning effect. In addition, beads and necklaces in vaseline shades catch the light beautifully.

Prices for vaseline have climbed steadily in recent years, in spite of the fact that this type of coloured glass was once considered the poor relation of other

Two Vaseline glass vases from £18 to £25 each; a 'tree trunk' vase in perfect condition £12–£15; two Vaseline glass necklaces. £25–£30 each

Silver-plated vesta case in the form of a book. Only £25 as the rather clumsily engraved initials on the small plaque devalue it

forms of Victorian decorative glass. A trumpet-like flower vase can be bought for £20–£25 (the trumpet shape seems to abound in vaseline), while a single 'tree trunk' vase may cost from only £12–£15, depending on its condition. Since such a variety of multi-branched vases was produced, it would be interesting to form a collection solely in this style.

Junk shops and flea markets are well worth visiting, and bring frequent rewards. A vaseline wall pocket was bought recently from a junk shop, the vendor swearing it was carnival glass, for only £12, and a string of vaseline beads was found at a flea market for £3.

In general, however, prices are similar to those for cranberry glass — starting from about £15, to several hundred pounds for an outstanding, hand-cut piece of attractive colour and twisted, intricate design.

VESTA CASES

These are match holders which were made for the large headed 'fusee' matches, or the small waxed lucifers. Each will have a ribbed band on it for striking the matches, and some had a metal ring at one end for suspending on a watch chain. They date from the mid-1800s through to the early part of the 20th century. Early matches were unstable and had to be contained safely.

They come in two types, the small oblong flat box, and the cylindrical type. The latter sometimes has a small holder into which a match could be inserted. This is called a 'Go To Bed', the idea being that a lighted match was placed in the holder and would last just long enough for the user to jump into bed before being plunged into darkness. The

boxes were always lidded, unlike the open
match holders made in figural form and
with a ribbed part for striking (see: *Match
Holders and Strikers*). They were made of
wood and shaped like bottles or barrels,
or had concentric rings for decoration,
and nearly all had a hole in the top for the
lighted match. Others were made in
brass, shaped and decorated much like
those in wood, but with the addition of
floral and geometric designs. Others could
be ivory, bone or tinplate. Prices will vary
from about £10 upwards.

Vesta cases — the small flat boxes —
were made in silver, plate, brass or other
metals with advertising slogan on such as
England's Glory Matches, wood
(including Mauchline and Tunbridgeware) and bakelite. They could also be in
novelty form such as a bottle of wine or a
lady's corset.

Silver cases are highly priced, costing
from about £30 for a very plain example
to about £200 for a circular vesta with a
pattern of three cyclists chased into the
silver.

They were also made in silver plate
and will cost from about £10,
undecorated, to about £40 for one
embossed with a portrait of Edward VII.
The shapes copied those made in silver
and, providing the plating is good, and not
worn or yellowed, are collectable.

*Silver-plated vesta case
with enamelled front
and back, and made as
a souvenir. £28*

VINAIGRETTES

These were small shallow boxes,
usually one by one and half inches,
with an inner pierced grille underneath in
which a sponge soaked in aromatic
vinegar was placed. They were popular in
the early 19th century, and silver
smithing techniques had so improved by
then that the Birmingham silversmiths

W

Silver vinaigrette with pretty embossing approximately 1¾ inches, some damage to the grille. £65

A postcard showing typical Louis Wain design. Small amount of damage to one corner. £4

were able to turn them out in great numbers.

Most vinaigrettes are rectangular, but occasionally they are heart-shaped or circular. Novelty shapes such as shells, shoes, acorns and purses were also made. The inner grille was pierced decoratively, perhaps with rosettes and scrollwork, floral patterns and leaves.

Usually of silver (although some glass perfume bottles had a small vinaigrette attached to the base), the vinaigrettes were intended to be carried in the pocket or purse, but some more decorative examples have a small ring attached for the user to suspend the vinaigrette on a chain.

Prices for ornate silver examples are high. This is because the vinaigrette was a delicate object and rough handling would damage the flimsy grille. Few have survived despite the large number made. A vinaigrette having a view of Windsor Castle in relief will cost over £200, but a plainer one with a small amount of decoration around the edge of the lid, dated 1801, will cost about £60–£80, and another with a tartan engraving dated 1847 will cost about the same price.

WAIN, LOUIS

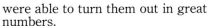

Born in 1860, Louis Wain will always be known as 'the man who drew cats', and his anthropomorphic cats are instantly recognizable. His greatest period of productivity was between 1890 and 1914 when he illustrated books, annuals, post cards, and painted pictures. Although he did draw other animals, it was the cat that made his name.

His first book was *The Kittens' Christmas Party* in 1886, and was closely followed by *Miss Tabby's Academy*. The cats were shown performing human activities such as shopping, golfing, playing cricket, going to the theatre, drinking tea, and relaxing on holiday at the seaside. Sometimes they were dressed as humans, sometimes as just cats.

Original pictures by Louis Wain fetch thousands of pounds, but early prints are collectable, and can be found in auction rooms and at antique fairs from about £20. Postcards are also eagerly sought and will start from about £12, although a recent find was a card bought for only £4 because a tiny piece was missing off one corner (see: *Postcards*). Children's books are a source for the collector, and it is worth examining annuals carefully in case one contains an early Louis Wain illustration.

He died in 1939, a victim of persecution mania, having spent many years in mental hospitals, and is buried in Kensal Green Cemetery.

WALKING STICKS

Victorian and later walking sticks and canes vary in price from about £5 for an unadorned example to over £200 for an ebony cane with an elaborate silver handle, so there is a great deal of scope for the beginner.

From the mid-1800s the standard cane of the time was made of Malacca, ebony or rosewood, the grip-type handle being made of gold or silver. An ebony example will cost about £80 today. It was not until the 1920s that the crook-handled walking stick made its appearance.

It is the handle that gives the cane its variety and appeal, and these can be found in carved ivory, or when wooden, can be in the shape of a horse's head, a Staffordshire bull terrier, birds, and even

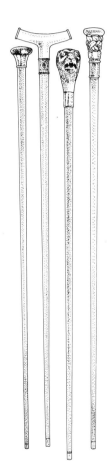

Four typical walking sticks ranging between £30 and £200

fairies, and these will cost about £60.

Novelty and gadget sticks were made. Racegoers would carry a stick containing a boxwood rule for measuring the height of a horse; fearful travellers used a sword stick, sporting enthusiasts could transform their sticks into fishing rods or billiard cues, while photographers used theirs as tripods. Compasses, street maps, and torches might be concealed in the handle. A sword stick will cost about £30, a measuring stick with boxwood rule will be about £50.

Sticks with a minimal amount of silver decoration can be bought from about £15, and plain walking sticks with very little decoration will be about £8–£12.

WATCH STANDS

At night, the Victorian gentleman would remove his watch and place it carefully on the watch stand beside his bed. These watch stands are now highly collectable, and were made in a variety of shapes, sizes and materials.

Wooden watch stands were made as boxes where the interior cut-out section would lift up and be held in a forty-five degree angled position for the watch to rest against it. Others had a circular base, a turned stem, and a round holder above lined with velvet to take the watch. These will cost between £30 and £40.

Cast watch stands were made in brass or iron, and can look like Gothic towers, or have elaborate winged panels, the watch being dropped into a rounded pocket-like container from behind. One cast metal stand has a street light illuminated with a pink shade, and a group of revellers below. The watch hangs just below the lamp and is

A Staffordshire watch stand in white, orange and cobalt blue. £70

illuminated when the battery operated light is switched on. This dates from the early 20th century and costs about £35.

Pottery and porcelain watch stands were also made, and a Staffordshire group has a pocket behind the aperture to take the watch. A Coalbrookdale stand is heavily encrusted with flowers and has a painted scene on the angled recess. This will cost between £70–£90.

Glass examples were made in box shapes — square or oval, and a stand with an oval cranberry glass base, the clear top magnifying the face of the watch, will cost about £60. Other variations are clear lidded boxes with angled interiors lined with silk, and these will be about £40.

A *papier mâché* watch stand is a simple board-like stand with a hook for the watch, and is decorated with flowers, and this will be about £20.

Silver stands resemble photograph frames, with heavy ornate embossing, and the watch rests against a velvet lining. Prices start at around £60–£70.

WEIGHTS

Victorian weights were made in brass, cast iron, and — more rarely seen — pottery. They were used domestically as well as commercially and vary in size from those measuring 1 lb through to 56 lbs and 8 ounces down to ¼ ounce. Dram weights went down to ¼ dram.

Brass weights were either bell weights — a waisted upright weight with a carrying handle on top — or flat circular weights which stacked neatly into one another and never weighed more than 7 lb. There were also cylindrical weights, having a knob on top to grasp for easier handling. Complete sets are expensive: a set of bell weights will cost £70–£90, but

Brass bell weights. The smaller one can be found from about £5, while larger versions are from £20 upwards

they can be bought singly from about £5.

Cast iron weights were also made in a flat, circular shape, or as a round 'bun'. Bar weights are squarish with integral handles, while another type of weight, wider at the base than at the top has an attached ring for use. A single iron weight of the latter shape can be bought for as little as £1 for a small size.

Pottery weights were soon discontinued as they were liable to chipping, and so losing weight, and an example of a 2 lb weight, slightly damaged, can cost as much as £20.

Cup weights were designed to fit into each other, building up into an angled upside-down dome. Encased in a metal holder, the smaller weight is always half the weight of the one it fits into. The lidded holder or cup should weigh as much as the remainder put together. Check that the smallest weight is present as these frequently went missing. A complete set will cost £30–£40.

WILLOW PATTERNED WARE

Davenport trio of cup, saucer and plate circa 1860. £30

A typical willow pattern will show three figures on an arched bridge, behind which is a pagoda flanked by an apple tree and a willow. A boat can be seen on the nearby river, a zig-zag fence in the foreground and two birds flying across the sky.

Most popular in blue and white, it can also be found in sepia, and later versions were made in pink (see: *Blue and White Transfer Printed Ware*). The picture represents the Chinese story of two lovers fleeing from the girl's father. They were going to escape by boat, but were caught. About to be put to death, the gods took pity on them and turned them into doves.

The first willow pattern was produced by Caughley in 1780, and other makers soon copied the design which became immensely popular. Early wares were usually dark blue, almost indigo, but as transfer printing improved, the colours became lighter.

Variations in the pattern make it interesting for the collector. The number of apples vary considerably; sometimes two figures are shown on the bridge, and not three, and on rare occasions there are no birds.

Fifty-four makers are known to have made the willow pattern ware and these have been identified, but countless unknown makers copied the pattern, and their wares are unmarked.

Plates are most sought after by collectors and some of these can be found reasonably priced when unmarked. For example, a 9-inch plate in dark blue was recently bought for £8; 10-inch plates will be from about £12.

Caughley tea plate, late 18th century. £35

WINE GLASSES

Before the advent of the superior lead glass — a discovery made by George Ravenscroft — most table glass was imported into Britain from the continent. But after 1675, with the new lead ingredient, English manufacturers excelled and by the 18th century drinking glasses were made in their thousands in Bristol, the Midlands, and the North-East. Glass was hand blown until about 1825 and close examination shows the striations in the glass indicative of hand blowing. Marks of wear on the foot will give indications of age, and variation in the stem is also an important feature in dating specimens.

The baluster and Silesian stems

Engraved sherry glass circa 1920. £6

date from 1725, air twist stems were
introduced in about 1745, faceted stems in
about 1770.

Baluster stems have a varying number
of knops, ranging from the single knop,
sometimes with a tear drop, to the eight
knopped bobbin stem. An example of one
of these costs over £200.

The air twist stem had many
variations, the pattern spiralling in
latticino style (see: *Paperweights*). Prices
start at about £60 for a simple example
with a multiple air twist stem. Faceted
stem glasses also start at about this price.

For collectors of more modest means,
Edwardian and later glass offers a great
deal of scope. Copies of 18th and early
19th century glass were made in the
1930s, and a whole set of wine glasses
can be collected piece by piece without
too much difficulty.

Machine-engraved glasses, with the
pattern on the base forming wavy
diamonds, with looped and floral
decorations, and scrolling on the rim, cost
about £4–£7 for a standard size. A suite
of matching glasses can be built up, as
these are still available in liqueur, port,
sherry and wine sizes, and small and large
tumblers. A Greek key pattern was a
popular motif, revived in the 1930s, and a
pattern of ovals swirling one on top of the
other (about half an inch below the rim of
the glass). Either of these patterns will
cost about £3 or £4 for a single glass.
Matching decanters can also be found and
will cost about £25.

Flashed glass, the pattern hand cut
into the coloured surface, is also to be
found, and a set of four was bought
recently for only £5. By sheer chance, a
matching set of four further glasses was
discovered only months later, but the
price was higher at £10.

*Fluted glass on faceted
stem. £30*

WINE LABELS

Known also as bottle tickets, wine labels were used primarily on decanters from about 1730. They were made in silver, enamel and porcelain, and later of silver plate, and hung around the neck of the container on a fine chain. Apart from late silver and silver plate, the prices will be beyond the reach of the average collector. For example, an early sherry label with shield insignia made in silver in 1775, will cost £200.

Silver-plated wine label. £10

Late 18th-century labels were decorated with bright-cutting (a method of engraving which faceted the silver into diamond-like patterns which caught and reflected the light). Feather edging was also used, as well as the technique of piercing.

The later development of die stamping meant that labels could be made in greater quantity at no extra cost and the industry flourished. Vine leaves appeared as a decoration in the early 19th century, sometimes adorned with bunches of grapes, the face of Bacchus, god of wine, and two attendant cherubs.

Sherry, port, claret, burgundy and madeira were usual, but one can find unusual labels such as Bucella or Calcavella (sweet white wines from Portugal), milk punch, British, Rhenish, Vin du Rhin, Hermitage and Barsac. The more unusual the label, the more expensive.

A silver label hallmarked 1809 adorned with bunches of grapes will cost about £80, as will an oval Madeira label surrounded by entwined vine leaves.

Silver plate labels are less expensive and will start at about £10 for a plain example. A more ornate label with the vine and leaf pattern, the name engraved in italics will cost about £25.

WOVEN BOOKMARKS & OTHERS

Victorian woven bookmark with a loving message. £12–£15

Thomas Stevens was the first person to put the new Jacquard looms to good use in about 1862 when he produced his woven pictures and bookmarks, the first bookmarker ribbon having being produced by John Caldicott. The bookmarkers were long strips of silk ribbon embroidered with flowers, scenes and messages. Some had Christmas or birthday greetings on them, such as Stevens' cream marker with a red tassel, bearing the words, 'This day once more I gladly hail, in memory of your birth. I wish you all the peace and joy that can be found on earth'. Caldicott markers included portrait heads of famous people and religious messages.

Silk bookmarkers are very collectable and one can expect to pay about £20; more for a Stevens marker.

Paper (card) bookmarkers are also collectable and still very cheap. A great many were issued by assurance companies, such as the Northern Assurance Company, the Friends Provident Institution, Bradford, and the Scottish Widow's Fund. (Look out for examples by Walter Crane.) These markers will cost from 40 pence to £2. A Boot's Book Lovers bookmark will cost about £5 — this shows a hand, fingers closed apart from an extended index finger. Another hand, this time fully extended and marked with palmistry symbols was issued by Fry's Chocolates and this is also £5.

Other novelty bookmarks were made such as Kolynos Dental Cream (a tube of toothpaste), St Ivel Cheese (a helmeted crusader holding a sword), Wisden's Exceller (a cricket bat), Lloyd's Weekly News (the head of a girl emerging from between the pages of a newspaper). These range in price between £2.50 and £7.50.

WRITING SLOPES

These were portable writing desks, and were intended to give a flat inclined surface when opened out. The top lid was made at an angle to the base, thus giving the required slope, and the interior was fitted with a leather covered board on which the writer could rest his paper. Beneath the lower board was a space for stationery or letters received, and in front of that was a pen rest with a space for nibs below, with an inkwell each side. The board in the lid of the box could be dropped open and more paper or envelopes could be kept behind it. Occasionally the slopes had a secret compartment, operated by a spring at the side of the box.

The slopes were made in mahogany, rosewood, coramandel, and satinwood. They sometimes had a brass shield or plate in the centre of the lid, and perhaps brass corner pieces. The key hole would be brass-edged. Prices range between £40 for a small Victorian slope to £80 for a larger slope in mahogany with two inkwells. A walnut box with a secret compartment will cost between £100–£140.

Check that the leather is in good condition, that the inkwells are not chipped at the base, and that the tops are not missing or mis-matched. The key should function, and the secret compartment swing open readily.

Mahogany writing slope with red leather interior. £60

INDEX

INDEX

INDEX

PICTURE CREDITS

'**Antique Collector**': 7(tl)
The Old Stables Antiques,
7(tc) Glen Dewart, 7(bl) Jean
Sewell, 7(br) Strawsons, 17, 21
John & Janet Simpson, 22, 26
Whitemarsh Antiques, 35(t)
Demas, 35(b) Cameo Corner,
36 Quinneys Jewellery, 37
Butterwalk House, 43
Grandads Photography
Museum, 49 Eureka, 51
Baynham Antiques, 58 Melvyn
Traub, 59, 62 Collectors
Corner, 63 Linda Bee, 64
Christies South Kensington,
65 Christies South Kensington,
66 Christies South Kensington,
69 Nigel Appleby & Lorna
Hanman, 70 Mcaskie, 79 The
Old Stables Antiques, 80
Caroline Ellert, 85(t) Turn
Again Antiques, 85(b) Browns
of Cheltenham, 86 Arden
House, 87 Arden House, 88(t)
Kingsbridge House Antiques,
89 Townley Antiques, 90
Naylors, 95, 98 Jean Sewell,
99 Britannia, 103 John & Janet
Simpson, 107 Pleasures of
Past Times, 108 Ellen Pollock
& Sister, 110 Paraphernalia,
113 Cobweb, 114 Taurus
Gallery, 115 Camera
Collection, 116 Glen Dewart,
117, 118 Hayman, 119
Langford, 123(t) Past Delights,
124(b), 126, 131 Jean Sewell,
132 Sadlers House, 133
Morgan Antiques, 134(t) The
Curio Shop, 135 Diane Harby,
136(t), 136(b) Sonia Cordell,
137, 138 Morgan Antiques,
143 J & R Day, 148 Melvyn
Traub, 149, 151 Asprey, 152(t)
Cobweb, 152(b) Sensation,
155(b) Orchard Antiques,
156(t,b), 159(b) Arden
Antiques, 160(t) Naylors,
164(t) The Little Window,
164(b), 165(t,b), 166(t)
R Harvey Morgan, 166(b),
167(t) Richmond Antiquary,
167(b) Regency House
Antiques, 168 MacMillan
Antiques, 169(b) The Curio
Shop, 170 Alyson Ager, 171(b)
Gooday, 172 Hayman, 178
Archer, 179 John & Janet
Simpson, 180(b) Finedon
Antique Centre, 182 1001
Treasures, 183 Glendale, 188
The Little Window, 189 John
Holmes, 190 Lynn's Antiques,
195 Guy Lemborelle, 200
Hasting Antique and Art
Centre, 201, 202(t), 202(b)
Atfield & Daughter, 204 Guy
Lemborelle, 206, 206(b) Turn
Again Antiques, 207 Robin &
Valerie Lloyd, 208 Wayside
Antiques, 209(t) O'Dwyer
Antiques, 209(b) Croesus,
211 Lamont Antiques, 212
Connaught Antiques, 213(t)
Guildhall Antiques, 213(b)
Chapman Antiques, 219
R S & S Negus, 221(t) Mrs
Joyce Archer, 221(b) Sonia
Cordell, 222 Joanne Warrand,
223(t) Jean Sewell, 223(b), 224,
225(t) Margaret E. Slade,
225(b), 226 Emmett, 227(t)
Linda Bee, 227(b) Audrey
Speight, 228 Naylors, 229(t)
Stephen Long, 229(b)
Stockspring Antiques, 231 Old
Woodworking Tools, 235
Strawsons, 236(t,b), 237
Rankin Best & Green, 238(b)
Burke, 239 Golden Past, 244
Sensation, 245(t) Connaught
Antiques, 245(b) Kingsbridge
House Antiques, 246. **City
Museum & Art Gallery**,
Stoke on Trent: 68, 192, 194,
203, 214, 215, 220. **The
Design Council**: 111, 112,
181, 193(t,b). **Mary Evans
Picture Library**: endpapers,
174(l,r), 248. **Poole Pottery**:
184. **Welsh Folk Museum**:
142. **All other photographs**
Peter Reilly. **Artwork** John
Hutchinson.

My thanks go to Catherine Cummings who gave me her invaluable assistance with the typing and checking of the manuscript.

I would also like to thank my many friends; collectors and dealers in the antiques trade, who gave me their time, the benefit of their experience, and their support in compiling this book. Here I would mention briefly: Dave Barker, Alan Benedick, Bernard's Heath Antiques, Frank and Shirley Fairs, Malcolm Davey, Colin Dixey, Pat and Ian Iremonger, Jessica Antiques, Auriol Miller, Molly, Pat and Josie Mulholland, Barry Muncey, Pamela and Barry Auctions, Trevor Pearson, and Peter.

My thanks too for the aid given by the Waterways Museum at Stoke Bruerne, and Shire Publications whose books have provided a valuable source of reference.

And last, but not least, my gratitude goes to Maggie and Tony for allowing me to make demands on their time, their knowledge, their collection of antiques, and their hospitality. *Muriel Miller*